Shoes for the Road

Richard H. Seume

moody press
chicago

To
Mary,
faithful companion
on the journey to
Palace Beautiful

© 1974 by
THE MOODY BIBLE INSTITUTE
OF CHICAGO

ISBN: 0-8024-7924-3

All scripture quotations in this book are from the King James
Version except where indicated otherwise.

The use of selected references from various versions of the
Bible in this publication does not necessarily imply publisher
endorsement of the versions in their entirety.

Printed in the United States of America

Contents

Prologue

IN HIS INCOMPARABLE ALLEGORY, *Pilgrim's Progress*, John Bunyan tells us that when the sisters of the Palace Beautiful led Christian to the armory, he saw such a bewildering abundance of boots as surely no other man ever beheld before or since! They were shoes that would never wear out! And there were enough of them, he says, to harness out as many men for the service of their Lord as there be stars in the heaven for multitude. Bunyan's prodigious stock of shoes is, of course, an allusion to Paul's exhortation to the believers at Ephesus concerning the armor with which he would have them clad. "Take unto you the whole armour of God," he wrote, "and [have] your feet shod with the preparation of the gospel of peace" (Eph 6:13, 15).

Referring to this matter, Frank W. Boreham makes two pertinent remarks in *Faces in the Fire*: "The man whose feet are shod with the preparation of the gospel of peace has carpeted for himself all the rough roads that lie before him. . . .He has already protected his feet against all the miry places of the path ahead of him." And yet, for all of that, Boreham adds this warning:

> The boots may have looked as though they would never wear out; but...I am really afraid that Christian was deceived in this particular. Paul says nothing about the everlasting wear of which the shoes are capable; and the sisters of the Palace Beautiful seem to have said nothing about it. I fancy Christian jumped too hastily to this conclusion, misled by the excellent appearance and sturdy make of the boots before him. My experience is that the shoes do wear out. The most "gracious, heavenly, and excellent spirit" must be kept in

5

repair. I know of no virtue, however attractive, and of no grace, however beautiful, that will not wear thin unless it is constantly attended to.[1]

It is the combination of this pair of propositions—shoes that will never wear out and yet which need to be kept in resolute repair lest they wear thin—which prompts this series of practical meditations. All of these "shoes," and more, have been observed on the feet of the saints of God along many roads of life and are worthy of a try on for size. If they fit, fine! They are shoes with a lifetime soul.

1
Are You a Gimper?

LONG BEFORE I had the term with which to express it, I had heard the truth about gimpers. The initial impression came through a remark by my esteemed friend, Howard W. Ferrin, who, on one occasion, said, "There is very little difference between men, but that little difference makes a very big difference." Immediately I found my heart and mind challenged in a new direction. As I examined my own life and observed those about me, I had to acknowledge that most of us are satisfied with mediocrity; we are content to be "tails"! Few there are among us who aspire to be different.

While I was thus musing, there came across my desk William Law's classic, *A Serious Call to a Devout and Holy Life*. There I discovered an illustration which spoke to the issue before me. It concerned a fictitious character named Penitens. As Law relates the story, it seems that Penitens was a busy, prosperous businessman who was faced with the hard fact that life was drawing to a close in his thirty-fifth year. Shortly before his death, when the doctors had given him over, some of his neighbors came to visit him and expressed their sorrow that one so young was being cut off in the prime of life. Penitens acknowledged their concern over his condition but spoke of his approaching demise with candor. He observed that the new experience before him made everything else in life completely trivial. It was just here that he made a startling confession. Said he,

> What a strange thing it is that a little health, or the poor business of the shop, should keep us so unaware of the great things that are coming upon us so fast! If I now had a thousand worlds I would give them all for one year of such

7

devotion and good works as I never so much as intended. . .
The thing that surprises me most is this: that I never
intended to live up to the Gospel. This never so much as
entered my head or heart. I never once considered whether I
was living as the laws of religion direct or whether my way of
life was such as would procure me the mercy of God at this
hour. What is the reason that I—who have so often talked of
the necessity of rules, methods, and diligence in worldly
business—have all this while never thought of any rules,
methods, or managements to carry me on in a life of devotion. Had I only my frailties and imperfections to lament at
this time I should lie here humbly trusting in the mercies of
God. But alas! How can I call a general disregard and a
thorough neglect of all religious improvement a frailty or
imperfection when it was in my power to have been as exact
and careful and diligent in a course of devotion as in the
business of my trade? I could have called in as many helps,
have practised as many rules, and have been taught as many
methods of holy living as of thriving in my shop, had I but so
intended and desired it.[1]

At this point, poor Penitens was interrupted by a convul-
sion which never permitted him to speak another word.

Despite the interruption, the convicting work was done in
my own heart, for I was confronted with the simple but
solemn truth that my friend of the page was all too typical of
most of us, myself included. We never really *intend* to im-
prove!

It was in this sequence of events that the Spirit of God
supplied the word for which I was, searching. It came
through reading a daily devotional in *Our Daily Bread* by M.
R. DeHaan. He it was who used for the first time, to my
knowledge, the word *gimper* and defined it as one who
aspires to excel. Evidently he based his definition on the
fact that the dictionary defines *gimp* as "ambition, spirit,
vigor." Taken together, they added up to my original impression that a gimper is one who aspires to be different.
He means business!

The Word of God provides a striking example of a gimper. The incident is recorded in a somewhat obscure passage in 1 Chronicles, chapter 4. In order to get the full impact of the Spirit's instruction, we must begin at the beginning of the chapter and read through the forty-one names which are catalogued without comment.

> The sons of Judah were Perez, Hezron, Carmi, Hur, and Shobal. And Reaiah the son of Shobal became the father of Jahath, and Jahath became the father of Ahumai and Lahad. These were the families of the Zorathites. And these were the sons of Etam: Jezreel, Ishma, and Idbash; and the name of their sister was Hazzelelponi. And Penuel was the father of Gedor, and Ezer the father of Hushah. These were the sons of Hur, the first-born of Ephrathah, the father of Bethlehem. And Ashhur, the father of Tekoa, had two wives, Helah and Naarah. And Naarah bore him Ahuzzam, Hepher, Temeni, and Haahashtari. These were the sons of Naarah. And the sons of Helah were Zereth, Izhar and Ethnan. And Koz became the father of Anub and Zobebah, and the families of Aharhel the son of Harum. And Jabez was more honorable than his brothers, and his mother named him Jabez saying, "Because I bore him with pain" (vv. 1-9, NASB).

Now, observe something remarkable. As soon as we reach verse nine, we become aware of a thrilling deviation: we are about to read the record of a gimper! Even the Holy Spirit seems to prepare us for this remarkable character, for we are told at the beginning of the verse, "Jabez was more honorable than his brothers." There was something different about him; the text says so! But wherein lay the difference? Not in his natural advantages, for his name suggests that he might have been something less than physically perfect. Nor was it to be found in any oustanding achievement. It was the *intention* of Jabez, as revealed in verse ten, that set him apart from his peers. Listen to this gimper's prayer: "Oh that Thou wouldst bless me indeed, and enlarge my border, and that Thy hand might be with me, and that Thou wouldst keep me from harm, that it may not pain me!"

It is not within my purpose here to obscure the main idea with an exposition of the prayer. I do want, however, to catch the spirit of the man as he poured out his heart to God. His desire for the divine blessing was specific; there was nothing vague about it. The land was his birthright, and Jabez wanted everything that was coming to him. He dared to say, "I am determined to be eternally wealthy." More than that, he coveted the hand of the Lord God in all areas of his life, especially where evil might threaten to turn him aside from the path of righteousness. It is all there in his prayer.

And did God answer His servant, His gimper friend? Hear these words, "And God granted him what he requested." This is but one instance in Scripture which assures us that God waits to be wanted! He delights to do business with those who mean business!

So much for the *example*.

This brings us to a word of *exhortation*.

In His initial sermon preached on the mount, our Lord had this to say, among other things:

> Love your enemies, bless them that curse you, do good to them that hate you, and pray for them which despitefully use you, and persecute you; that ye may be the children of your Father which is in heaven: for he maketh his sun to rise on the evil and on the good. . . .For if ye love them which love you, what reward have ye? do not even the publicans the same? And if ye salute your brethren only, what do ye more than others? do not even the publicans so? (Mt 5:44-47).

How To Love

The word which stands out in that text, insofar as our purpose is concerned, is in verse forty-seven, "What do ye *more* than others?" Here is the personal challenge to any of us who would be numbered among God's gimpers.

What do we more than others in our *personal* life?

What do we more than others in our *domestic* life?

What do we more than others in our *social* life?
What do we more than others in our *business* life?
What do we more than others in our *spiritual* life?
You see at once the question opens the door to the house
and all its rooms. We are challenged to apply it to anything
and everything that is worthwhile in the life of the Christian
who really intends to please the Lord and serve his generation by the will of God.
This poem, appropriately entitled "The Second Mile,"
serves to underscore the truth.

"Come here, you dog, and bear my pack a mile."
So spoke a Roman soldier to a Jew;
"The day is hot, and I would rest the while—
Such heavy loads were made for such as you."

The Jew obeyed, and, stopping in the path,
He took the burden, though his back was tired;
For who would dare arouse a Roman's wrath,
Or scorn to do what Roman law required?

They walked the mile in silence; at its end
They paused, but there was not a soul in sight;
"I'll walk another mile with you, my friend,"
Spoke up the Jew, "This burden now seems light."

"Have you gone mad?" the angry Roman cried,
"To mock me, when you know that but one mile
Can I compel such service?" By his side
The Jew stood silent, but with kindly smile.

"I used to hate to bear a Roman's load,
Before I met the lowly Nazarene,
And walked with Him along the dusty road,
And saw Him make the hopeless leper clean.

"I heard Him preach a sermon on the mount;
He taught that we should love our enemies;

He glorified the little things that count
So much in lessening life's miseries."

The soldier tried to speak; as he began
His head was bowed, his eyes with tears were dim;
"For many years I've sought for such a man,
Pray tell me more. I, too, would follow Him."

JOSEPH E. HARVEY

It remains now for us to say a word about the *encouragement* in this meditation. There is a word of encouragement, and again it comes from the lips of our Lord as He related the familiar story of the good Samaritan. The encouragement is in connection with the Samaritan's comment to the innkeeper concerning the welfare of the beaten and bruised man and his charge to him: "Take care of him; and whatsoever thou spendest *more*, when I come again, I will repay thee" (Lk 10:35).

Here is a gracious promise to all gimpers! As the Lord's dear children, called to serve Him in so many needy areas of this world, let us never forget that whatever it costs, whatever we spend *more* in loving concern and care toward the completion of our commission, He will repay in that day when we stand at the judgment seat of Christ and are rewarded for faithful service.

Perhaps it was of gimpers that Amy Carmichael was thinking when she wrote those well-known lines bearing the title, "Make me Thy Fuel."[2] Wrote that honored servant of the Saviour;

From prayer that asks that I may be
Sheltered from winds that beat on Thee,
From fearing when I should aspire,
From faltering when I should climb higher,
From silken self, O Captain, free
Thy soldier who would follow Thee.

(margin handwriting: THE ENCOURAGEMENT FOR A GIMPER)

From subtle love of softening things,
From easy choices, weakenings—
Not thus are spirits fortified;
Not this way went the Crucified.
From all that dims Thy Calvary,
O Lamb of God, deliver me.

Give me love that leads the way,
The faith that nothing can dismay,
The hope no disappointments tire,
The passion that will burn like fire.
Let me not sink to be a clod;
Make me Thy fuel, flame of God.

Read them again, and see if your heart does not think of gimpers. And then, may it please God that each of us will rise from our reading to pray, "O God, make *me* Thy gimper!"

2
The Vital Vision

"TRAFFICKING in unfelt truth is dangerous business."

These words were spoken over thirty years ago by the well-known and beloved pastor of the Moody Church, Henry Allen Ironside. At the time I heard them, I felt they must be true, because he had said them. But the passing years spent in the laboratory of the pastorate have assured me that they *are* true. One cannot but sense a very wide gulf between the spiritual knowledge of God's people and their spiritual experience, between what they believe and how they behave.

Some years ago, this fact was brought home to my own heart while attending a gathering of college young people. When opportunity was given for personal witness, one young woman acknowledged her situation in these words: "Academically, I am a junior in college, but spiritually, I feel like a high school senior." I could not but admire her honesty and at the same time admit to myself that this is the condition with most of us who call ourselves Christians.[1]

For our encouragement, however, let us remember that this is not a new problem. The children of Israel knew more than they had experienced. They knew about the promised land, but it took them a whole generation to experience it! It was only then that the summons came to young Joshua, "Moses my servant is dead; now therefore arise, go over this Jordan, thou, and all this people, unto the land which I do give to them, even to the children of Israel. Every place that the sole of your foot shall tread upon, that have I given unto you, as I said unto Moses" (Jos 1:2-3).

We must remember, further, that the structure of the Scripture itself anticipates this hiatus. For example, in reading many of the epistles, one is aware of two equally vital thrusts. The first is in the direction of positional truth—setting forth what we *are* in Christ; the second is in the direction of practical truth—what we *ought to be* because of what we are. This explains the language of the apostle Paul to the church at Ephesus. After declaring the fact of their wealth in Jesus Christ, he moves at once to exhort them: "I therefore, the prisoner of the Lord, beseech you that ye walk worthy of the vocation wherewith ye are called" (Eph 4:1).

In a word, then, our perennial need is for an updating of our Christian experience so that it is relevant to our lives. Here is an indispensable shoe, and it needs to be kept in constant repair.

But where does one begin this spiritual pilgrimage? Where is our basic need? Surely the answer to that question lies in the realm of our relationship to the Lord Jesus Christ. And no one has verbalized it more practically and perceptively than Horatius Bonar, who wrote:

> To know the Christ of God,
>   The everlasting Son;
> To know what He on earth
>   For guilty man has done;
> This is the first and last
>   Of all that's true and wise;
> The circle that contains all light
>   Beneath, above the skies.
>
> The Christ, the incarnate Son,
>   The Christ, the eternal Word;
> The Christ, heaven's glorious King,
>   The Christ, earth's coming Lord.
> The Christ, the sum of all
>   Jehovah's power and grace,
> God's treasure-house of truth,
>   The brightness of His face.

The Christ who took man's flesh,
Who lived man's life below;
Who died man's death for man,
The death of shame and woe.
The Christ who from the cross
Descended to man's grave,
Then rose in victory and joy,
Mighty to bless and save!

Father, unseal my eyes,
Unveil my veiled heart,
Reveal *this Christ to me*!

With this prayer on our lips and in our hearts and minds, let us give attention to some familiar words in the first chapter of the book of the Revelation, where we have one of the most complete and compelling unveilings of our Lord to be found anywhere in Scripture. The setting is worthy of notice. John, the beloved apostle, was on the island called Patmos, "for the word of God, and for the testimony of Jesus Christ" (v. 9). He was not there as a sightseer. And yet, what a sight he saw! It pleased the Lord to reveal Himself to His servant in such a manner as you and I need Him to reveal Himself to us in our generation.

Observe, in the first place, the *position* of the Lord Jesus in John's revelation. John writes, "And I turned to see the voice that spake with me. And being turned, I saw seven golden candlesticks; and in the midst of the seven candlesticks one like unto the Son of man" (Rev 1:12-13). We are told at the end of this same chapter that the seven candlesticks are the seven churches. And where is He in relation to those churches? *In the midst!* And to confirm our position, to make it even more solemn, we read these words at the beginning of chapter 2, verse 1: "These things saith he that holdeth the seven stars in his right hand, who walketh in the midst of the seven golden candlesticks." Not only is He in the midst, but He is *walking* in the midst.

What a solemn thought indeed! How searching! No aisle is too narrow for Him to pass through. No pew too remote for Him to find. No congregation too small or large for His scrutiny. And no pulpit, I might add, which He is not free to share with the pastor.

Perhaps this personal testimony from the pen of A. J. Gordon, for many years the esteemed shepherd of Boston's Clarendon Street Baptist Church, provides the window on this truth.

It was Saturday night, when wearied from the work of preparing Sunday's sermon, that I fell asleep and the dream came. I was in the pulpit before a full congregation, just ready to begin my sermon, when a stranger entered and passed slowly up the left aisle of the church looking first to the one side and then to the other as though silently asking with his eyes that someone would give him a seat. He had proceeded nearly half-way up the aisle when a gentleman stepped out and offered him a place in his pew, which he quietly accepted. Excepting the face and the features of the stranger, everything in the scene is distinctly remembered—the number of the pew, the Christian man who offered its hospitality, the exact seat which was occupied. . . .Immediately as I began my sermon my attention became riveted on this hearer. If I would avert my eyes from him for a moment they would instinctively return to him, so that he held my attention rather than I held his till the discourse was ended.

To myself I said constantly, "Who can that stranger be?" and then I mentally resolved to find out by going to him and making his acquaintance as soon as the service should be over. But after the benediction had been given the departing congregation filed into the aisles and before I could reach him the visitor had left the house. The gentleman with whom he sat remained behind however; and approaching him with great eagerness I asked: "Can you tell me who that stranger was who sat in your pew this morning?" In the most matter-of-course way he replied: "Why, do you not know that man? It was Jesus of Nazareth." With a sense of the keenest disappointment I said: "My dear sir, why did you let him go without introducing me to him?" And with the same nonchalant air the gentleman replied: "Oh, do not be troubled. He has been here today, and no doubt he will come again."

And now came an indescribable rush of emotion, as when a strong current is suddenly checked, the stream rolls back upon itself and is choked in its own foam, so the intense curiosity which had been going out toward the mysterious hearer now returned upon the preacher. . . .What was I saying? Was I preaching on some popular theme in order to catch the ear of the public?...In what spirit did I preach?...Other questions began with equal vehemence to crowd into the mind. "What did he think of our sanctuary, its gothic arches, its stained windows, its costly and powerful organ? How was he impressed with the music and the order of the worship?" It did not seem at that moment as though I could ever again care or have the smallest curiosity as to what men might say of preaching, worship, or church, if I could only know that he had not been displeased, that he would not withhold his feet from coming again because he had been grieved at what he might have seen or heard.[1]

You will not be surprised to learn that A. J. Gordon's ministry was transformed after that experience, even though it was only a dream. The presence of the living Christ in the midst of the church became awesomely relevant to the preacher.

This is a word in season to all of us. Those of us who minister in any area of Christian service should always seek to minister in the context of Christ's presence. History tells us that the skeptic David Hume used to say of John Brown of Haddington, "Yon's the man for me: he preaches as if Jesus Christ were at his elbows!" And to those of you who are ministered to, that presence should be equally remembered. You can best answer for yourself by asking the obvious questions: Did He find me in my place last Lord's Day? Was I actively involved in the worship, sharing in the singing, having my proportionate share in the material needs of the church, giving earnest heed to the message as it was delivered?

It is my firm conviction that when the Church of God remembers the place of her Lord in her midst, her worship within and her witness without will more nearly conform to the pattern given in the holy mount.

But take another look at our text. Observe this time the *portrait* which John draws of Jesus Christ. Writing of Him, he says, "His head and his hairs were white like wool, as white as snow; and his eyes as a flame of fire; and his feet like unto fine brass, as if they burned in a furnace; and his voice as the sound of many waters. And he had in his right hand seven stars: and out of his mouth went a sharp two-edged sword: and his countenance was as the sun shineth in his strength" (Rev 1:14-16).

When did you last see the Lord Jesus Christ like that? Ever?

For much too long now, most of us have been content with the childhood impression made upon our minds by that harmless couplet,

> Gentle Jesus, meek and mild,
> Look upon a little child.

Or we image Him as the lowly Galilean as He walked this earth in the days of His flesh. I am not denying His humanity, for it was a vital part of the incarnation invasion; but I do affirm the fact that a biblical view of the Saviour sees Him as John saw Him. Nothing less! Anything less, and our God is too small! He stands before us in John's portrait as the mature, pure, austere, authoritative, supreme, discerning, vigorous Man in the glory. That is how He is now. And that is how we see Him with the eye of faith, if indeed we really do see Him at all.

As one observes the Church in worship and at work, one cannot but wonder. Perhaps J. H. Jowett was right when he wrote,

> We leave our places of worship, and no deep and inexpressible wonder sits upon our faces. . . .There is nothing about us to suggest that we have been looking at anything stupendous

and overwhelming. Far back in my boyhood I remember an old saint telling me that after some services he liked to make his way home alone, by quiet by-paths, so that the hush of the Almighty might remain on his awed and prostrate soul."[2]

It was thus with the great Puritans, men who, in Macaulay's classic phrase, "were not content to catch occasional glimpses of the Deity through an obscuring veil, but aspired to gaze full on His intolerable brightness and commune with Him face to face."

Do not these thoughts cause us to pray with Bonar, "Reveal this Christ to me"?

But there is one further thought in our text before the vision is complete. We have marked our Lord's position in the Church. We have looked briefly and beggarly at His portrait. It remains now for us to consider the *purpose* for which He takes His place in the midst of the Church.

You will remember that on one occasion, when our Lord was debating with the Jews, He made this statement, "the Father judgeth no man, but hath committed all judgment unto the Son" (Jn 5:22). And a little later in that same chapter, He went on to say, "For as the Father hath life in himself; so hath he given to the Son to have life in himself; and hath given him authority to execute judgment also, because he is the Son of man" (vv. 26-27).

Now, the point is that as we see the risen Christ in John's apocalypse, He appears in the vestments of that judicial responsibility committed to Him by His Father, "clothed with a garment down to the foot, and girt about the paps with a golden girdle" (Rev 1:13).

What is He doing? The Son of Man is walking in the midst of the Church for the purpose of judging the Church! His own words confirm this. To each of the seven churches He speaks these words, "I know thy works. . . .I know thy works. . . .I know thy works." Nothing either good or bad is hidden from His eyes; He sees it all! Little wonder that someone has described this scene as the "judicial verdict of the Son of Man." So it is.

And little wonder that John was so deeply affected by what he saw and heard. He confesses in verse 17, "And when I saw him, I fell at his feet as dead." I should think so! The realization of the meaning of the vision became relevant to John's tender heart, and he found being on his knees the only comfortable posture.

A. W. Tozer, that prophet of the Christian and Missionary Alliance, once wrote as from the throne itself, "If we would bring back spiritual power to our lives, we must begin to think of God more nearly as He is." This, my friends, will mean a relevant revelation of Jesus Christ to our own lives. With that vital vision before us and the example of the apostle for our encouragement, let us take whatever steps are necessary, even if they are costly. Let us do any amount of housecleaning or overhauling, so that we may see the King in His beauty and be the men and women of spiritual power which our generation so desperately needs.

3
A Second Glance

IN THE PREVIOUS MEDITATION, we sought to establish a broad base of common need among believers for a personal updating in the matters of Christian knowledge and experience. Upon that base we erected the vital superstructure of the Lord Jesus Christ, whose position, portrait, and purpose we found to be intimately related to everyone who bears His dear name. In fact, we learned the inescapable truth that He knows all about us!

That truth has a twin!

Reflecting for a moment on the record of the Old Testament, you will recall that when the presence of the living God became real to the patriarch Job, he cried, "I have heard of thee by the hearing of the ear: but now mine eye seeth thee. Wherefore I abhor myself, and repent in dust and ashes" (Job 42:5-6). And when the prophet Isaiah saw the Lord high and lifted up, he confessed unashamedly, "Woe is me! for I am undone; because I am a man of unclean lips. . . for mine eyes have seen the King, the LORD of hosts" (Is 6:5). It was even thus with Daniel, whose piety earned him insight into some of the deepest things of prophecy. When he saw the vision of that certain man, he acknowledged, "There remained no strength in me: for my comeliness was turned in me into corruption, and I retained no strength" (Dan 10:8).

What do these texts combine to teach us? They teach us that when true men of God saw the Lord as He is, they saw themselves as they were! And the sight was not flattering!

But some are certain to ask, Do these experiences find a counterpart in the New Testament? Is it not so that things

22

are different now, in this dispensation of grace? Has there not been a marked improvement in the human heart since the days of the patriarchs and the prophets?

We have an answer to these questions from the New Testament, and the answer comes from one who was eminently qualified to speak for us all. Bunyan would have called him "Mr. Christian." We know him as Paul the apostle. In revealing his innermost heart to the saints at Rome, he wrote,

> For I know that in me (that is, in my flesh,) dwelleth no good thing: for to will is present with me; but how to perform that which is good I find not. For the good that I would I do not: but the evil which I would not, that I do. Now if I do that I would not, it is no more I that do it, but sin that dwelleth in me. I find then a law, that, when I would do good, evil is present with me. For I delight in the law of God after the inward man: But I see another law in my members, warring against the law of my mind, and bringing me into captivity to the law of sin which is in my members. O wretched man that I am! Who shall deliver me from the body of this death? (Ro 7:18-24).

Without attempting a close analysis of these verses, which would be outside the purpose of this study, let us consider for a moment the two basic discoveries which came to the apostle at this critical point in his life as a believer. First, and obvious, was the discovery of *defeat*. Only a chapter earlier, Paul had developed at length the truth of the destiny of holiness for every believer, based upon the death and resurrection of Christ. He had reminded his readers of this destiny in such familiar words as these: "As ye have yielded your members servants to uncleanness and to iniquity unto iniquity; even so now yield your members servants to righteousness unto holiness" (Ro 6:19). Holiness, then, is a true goal of the child of God. But in the application of that vital truth in his own life, Paul discovered that he was hopelessly defeated, and he admitted it! While he wanted desperately to attain the purpose for which he knew he had been converted, he learned to his dismay that holiness without help was impossible!

There was another discovery which badgered him—not only his defeat, but his *depravity* as well. In essence, the apostle became aware of the presence of the sin nature and its bias toward evil in his own life. And for the moment, he did not know the way out. It was under the weight and discovery of these things that he cried, "O wretched man that I am! who shall deliver me from the body of this death?"

It is just here that we ask ourselves the question, How did Paul arrive at this discovery? By an honest recognition of two antagonists in his life. He identifies the first in verse 22: "For I delight in the law of God after the inward man." The phrase "the inward man" is peculiar to Paul and appears in only two other places, 2 Corinthians 4:16 and Ephesians 3:16.

Who is this inward man? Taking the texts referred to above together, it seems clear that this speaks of the new nature which Paul received at the moment the blow of God was inflicted upon his fanatical soul en route to Damascus. For *that man* in him, there was immediate response to the word of the risen Christ to him. Rising to his feet, blind and groping, helpless as a little child, the new convert became the prisoner of the Lord forever! Now he could sing:

> The proudest heart that ever beat,
> Hath been subdued in me
> The wildest will that ever rose
> To scorn Thy cause, or aid Thy foes
> Is quelled my God, by Thee!
>
> Thy will, and not my will be done,
> Henceforth I'd be forever Thine,
> Confessing Thee, the Living Word,
> My Savior, Christ, my God, my Lord,
> Thy Cross shall be my sign.[1]
>
> W. HONE

But as genuine as that experience was, the spiritual conflict was not finished, for in verse 23 the apostle acknowledges the other antagonist: "But I see another law in my members, warring against the law of my mind, and bringing me into captivity to the law of sin which is in my members." Who is this culprit? Something which answers to the name "my members." And what can that mean? None other but the old nature, with all its original drive and drag upon the man of God, leading not only to defeat but to an acute awareness of a depraved nature.

Make no mistake about it, sin was real to the apostle Paul.

Let us pause just here to ask ourselves a few questions. Have we discovered our own hearts in this way? Has sin become so real to us that we can say from personal experience, "I know that in me, that is, in my flesh, there dwells no good thing"? I grant you, this is almost a forgotten experience today. As Vance Havner has written,

> In this age, when too often the church is but a mutual admiration society, when man is thought to need polish instead of pardon, when dainty little theories of "living like Jesus" supplant the old dynamite sermons on sin and grace, praise God if now and then some mortal gets a right view of inward depravity and cries, "Woe is me! for I am undone!" It is a sign that you are beginning to see sin as God sees it, and therefore God is working in you.[2]

"Blessed downcastings that drive us to Thee, O Lord," was Charles Spurgeon's way of saying it. In either case, it is a glance for good. Downcastings there are. Both Testaments have demonstrated this fact, and our own experience confirms the truth that none of us is without sin. And the closer we get to the Lord Jesus Christ, the more we realize this.

But, thank God, there is *deliverance* from our downcastings! There is an answer to Paul's cry of agony. Consider three secrets to victory over sin in the believer's life.

First, deliverance from sin's power is possible through the Word of God. Again and again, the Bible promises victory over sin to those who will hear and heed its message. "Thy word have I hid in mine heart," wrote David in Psalm 119:11, "that I might not sin against thee." In summoning the saints at Ephesus to "be strong in the Lord, and in the power of his might" (Eph 6:10), Paul includes in the list of equipment for warfare "the sword of the Spirit, which is the word of God" (Eph 6:17). And the aged apostle John finds reason to compliment the young men to whom he writes, because "the word of God abideth in you, and ye have overcome the wicked one" (1 Jn 2:14).

Is it any surprise, then, that Bunyan wrote these words in the flyleaf of his Bible—words which have been written many times since—"This Book will keep you from sin, or sin will keep you from this Book."

As I have been privileged to counsel with God's people over the years, I have come to the settled conclusion that neglect of the Word of God is the first wrong turn in the road and leads to defeat and failure in the Christian life. The Bible contains our heavenly Father's love letters to us, and when we ignore them, we do so at our own spiritual peril and loss.

There is a second secret. I speak now of the Spirit of God. Returning, for a moment, to our earlier consideration of Romans, chapters 6 and 7, you will remember that we said that the first of these chapters sets forth the destiny of holiness as the birthright of every believer. But as we pointed out further, from Paul's own testimony in chapter 7, the teacher failed his own examination. He learned that there was a difficulty in attaining that holiness. Paul discovered that he needed help from another source. Once he turned away from himself and looked off to the hills for help, he discovered the dynamic of holiness, the Holy Spirit Himself! It is worthy of note that when the apostle reaches chapter 8 in the Roman letter, he refers to that blessed Companion no less than eighteen times! He it is who delivers from the flesh. He it is who declares our adoption. He it is who delights to help us.

Is it any wonder that others who have walked this road

before us and made this discovery have put their testimony in song? Who among us does not delight to sing on occasion,

> Holy Spirit, Faithful Guide,
> Ever near the Christian's side;
> Gently lead us by the hand,
> Pilgrims in a desert land;
> Weary souls fore'er rejoice,
> While they hear that sweetest voice
> Whisp'ring softly, "Wand'rer, come!
> Follow Me, I'll guide thee home."
>
> MARCUS M. WELLS

And so He will.

And now for a closing thought. Deliverance from sin is possible for the believer because we have the Word of God *to* us; we have the Spirit of God *in* us; and finally, we have the Son of God *for* us. We read in Hebrews, "For Christ is not entered into the holy places made with hands. . .but into heaven itself, now to appear in the presence of God for us" (Heb 9:24).

What a comforting truth to the heart of the Christian. The nearer we get to the realization of our position and inheritance in Christ, the more we appreciate that there stands One in the eternal presence of God Himself who, because of the eternal value of His sacrifice for sin, is able to meet every argument leveled against us. Such a thought calls to mind some words passed on to me years ago, now, and bearing the simple title, "My Advocate."

> I sinned. And straightway, posthaste, Satan flew
>   Before the presence of the most high God,
> And made a railing accusation there. He said,
>   "This soul, this thing of clay and sod,
> Has sinned. 'Tis true that he has named Thy name,
>   But I demand his death, for Thou hast said,
> 'The soul that sinneth, it shall die.' Shall not
>   Thy sentence be fulfilled? Is justice dead?
> Send now this wretched sinner to his doom.

What other thing can righteous ruler do?"
And thus he did accuse me day and night,
   And every word he spoke, O God, was true!

Then quickly One rose up from God's right hand,
   Before whose glory angels veiled their eyes.
He spoke, "Each jot and tittle of the law
   Must be fulfilled; the guilty sinner dies!
But wait! Suppose his guilt were all transferred
   To Me, and I paid his penalty!
Behold My hands, My feet, My side! One day
   I was made sin for him, and died that he
Might be presented faultless at Thy throne!"
   And Satan flew away. Full well he knew
That he could not prevail against such love,
   For every word my dear Lord spoke was true!

AUTHOR UNKNOWN

    The apostle John gave us the last word on this vital truth when he wrote, "My little children, these things write I unto you, that ye sin not. And if any man sin, we have an advocate with the Father, Jesus Christ the righteous: and he is the propitiation for our sins: and not for ours only, but also for the sins of the whole world" (1 Jn 2:1-2).

4

A Declaration of Dependence

IT WAS SUNDAY MORNING. I had been invited to minister in the pulpit of one of our seminary graduates in a lovely church fellowship. As I sat on the platform and the service unfolded, there was a certain uneasiness about the message to be delivered. Just before the pastor introduced me, we sang together Charles Wesley's familiar hymn, "Love Divine, All Loves Excelling." It was the second verse that spoke to my heart and gave me the launching site for the sermon that morning. Those words, so well known, came through fresh and challenging:

> Breathe, O breathe Thy loving Spirit
> Into every troubled breast!
> Let us all in Thee inherit,
> Let us find that second rest.

That second rest! That was it! That was what I must preach about. And I did, and with the conviction then, as now, that it forms one of those vital links in the chain of the Christian life. It is another shoe!

When we come to Jesus Christ to receive Him as personal Saviour, we enter that *first* rest. Perhaps no text speaks more particularly to the point than Matthew 11:28, "Come unto me, all ye that labour and are heavy laden, and I will give you rest." This He does give—rest from the struggle with sin and its blight upon the human heart. But while this blessed experience does deal with our *sins*, working forgiveness and justification, it does not destroy *ourselves*. We are still possessed of our old nature, with its Adamic posture and

29

purpose to assert itself. Now, if our Christian experience is to be relevant here, the time must inevitably come, sooner or later, when God steps in and deals with this part of us. For not only is our independence contrary to His divine claim upon our lives, but it actually threatens our usefulness! God cannot truly bless us until He breaks us!

The Word of God provides, in the life of Jacob, a striking illustration of this whole operation. The story of God's personal and special dealings with Jacob commences with an incident recorded in Genesis, chapter 28. The chapter opens in an atmosphere of farewells. Isaac and Rebecca were giving their son final words of counsel before he left them to seek his fortune in another land. It is almost certain that this was Jacob's first time away from home.

Sometime after his departure, Jacob arrived at Bethel, and because the sun was going down, and the swift, Eastern darkness was approaching, he decided to spend the night there. Influenced, no doubt, by his surroundings, Jacob thought that the stone which he used for a pillow seemed like stairs reaching from earth to heaven, with the angels of God ascending and descending upon them. As Griffith Thomas surveyed this scene long ago, he wrote,

> The ladder was intended first of all to remind Jacob of the gulf between his soul and God. By craft he had obtained his brother's birthright, by lying and deceit he had snatched away the blessing, and now the fugitive is reminded of the separation between his soul and God and the absolute necessity of some means of communication. The ladder also reminded him of the way in which his soul could come back to God in spite of his sin, and the fact that it reached from earth to heaven signified the complete provision of Divine grace for human life. Right down to his deepest need the ladder came, right up to the presence of God the ladder reached, and the vision of the angels on the ladder was intended to symbolize the freedom of communication, telling of access to God, and of constant, free, easy communication between earth and heaven.[1]

It was at this point that the symbolic became specific, and Jacob heard the voice of the Lord speaking to him, and saying,

> I am the LORD God of Abraham thy father, and the God of Isaac: the land whereon thou liest, to thee will I give it, and to thy seed; and thy seed shall be as the dust of the earth, and thou shalt spread abroad to the west, and to the east, and to the north, and to the south: and in thee and in thy seed shall all the families of the earth be blessed. And, behold, I am with thee, and will keep thee in all places whither thou goest, and will bring thee again into this land; for I will not leave thee, until I have done that which I have spoken to thee of (Gen 28:13-15).

Observe, in passing, the remarkable evidences of divine sovereignty undergirding these promises. There is nothing in the language of men quite as impressive as God's "I will."

It is clear from what follows this divine pronouncement that Jacob was impressed. Apparently he had not had any personal encounter with God prior to this incident. But once the Lord revealed Himself to His servant, he confessed, "Surely the LORD is in this place." Yet, as blessed as that experience was, Jacob continued to carry something in his nature which was hard and unconquered. It lingered, year upon year. For nearly twenty years he ranged near and far, proving to himself and to all who came in contact with him that he was still the "old master of applied psychology learned the hard way." Jacob's way it was!

This brings us at last to Genesis, chapter 32. It is interesting to note the words with which this chapter opens; they are so characteristic of Jacob at this time. "And Jacob went on his way." It was Jacob's way, all right, but the road was narrowing to a single lane, and within hours he would face the crisis of his life. As he neared the borders of the old country, memory became active; conscience began to convict. He knew there could be no peace until his relationship with his brother, Esau, was made right. But how to do it! That was Jacob's dilemma.

As a trial gesture, Jacob dispatched messengers to his brother. But when they returned, they only confirmed his fears; Esau was coming to meet him with four hundred men! Whatever Esau meant to accomplish by such a formidable retinue is not clear, but it had the immediate effect of driving Jacob to take up once again the work he knew so well— scheming! He divided his possessions into two groups, so that in the event Esau fell on one of them, the other might escape. And as a final act of caution—so he schemed—he sent his family over the ford Jabbok and determined to spend the fateful night alone. The one absorbing thought in Jacob's mind was his meeting with his brother; it never seemed to occur to him that there was another appointment, his meeting with God!

But make no mistake about it. That appointment had been scheduled in heaven, and under the cover of that dark and lonely night, Jacob was suddenly conscious of an assailant. "There wrestled a man with him," the story goes. Mind you, Jacob was not wrestling with the heavenly visitor; this was God at work with Jacob! In the words of another, "He had a controversy with this double-dealing and crafty child of His; desirous to break up his self-sufficiency forever, and to give scope for the development of the Israel that lay cramped and coffined within."

For a time, the "wily old heel-catcher" held his own in the struggle. At last, however, when the heavenly assailant saw that he could not prevail against his friend, he touched the hollow of Jacob's thigh, and in one swift but certain stroke took away the very power required for wrestling; and Jacob was rendered helpless.

It is well for us to take note just here that whatever it may be which stands in the way of the Lord's blessing in our lives, He will touch it in His own time and way. There is nothing vague about His dealings with us in such matters.

It was so with our friend. Disabled at the very point of his former strength, Jacob could do nothing now but cling. From cunning to clinging—this was the experience of crafty

Jacob. Broken at last he was ready for the blessing. "I will not let thee go except thou bless me," he cried. He got it! In reality, he got more than he asked for, for as we examine the closing verses carefully, we discover that Jacob got three things. He got a new name, for God said, "Thy name shall be called no more Jacob, but Israel" (v. 28). He also got a new power, for in that same verse God said, "As a prince hast thou power with God and with men, and hast prevailed." And he got a new vision. In verse 30, Jacob testifies, "I have seen God face to face, and my life is preserved."

How beautifully Charles Wesley, whose hymn spawned this meditation in the first place, caught the rare atmosphere of this particular scene when he wrote as though from the thoughts of Jacob:

> My strength is gone, my nature dies;
>   I sink beneath Thy weighty hand;
> Faint to revive, and fall to rise:
>   I fall, and yet by faith I stand.
> I stand, and will not let Thee go,
>   Till I thy name, Thy nature know.
>
> Lame as I am, I take the prey;
>   Hell, earth, and sin, with ease o'ercome;
> I leap for joy, pursue my way,
>   And as a bounding hart fly home,
> Through all eternity to prove,
>   Thy nature and Thy name is love.

And as he passed over Penuel, the story ends, "The sun rose upon him, and he halted upon his thigh." What a spectacle of sheer beauty! Despite his limp, his was the posture of power. He was Israel now! He was God's own prince now! He had been to the mountain and had seen the vision of the Almighty! But do not forget this, it took a breaking to bring it to pass.

Such was Jacob's crisis at Jabbok. There he surrendered up his arms and declared his dependence.

But this meditation can become meaningful for us only when we allow the Spirit of God to press home this question to our hearts: Are we surrendered to Jesus Christ? Gladly we have received the *gift* element in the gospel. And we can quote the Scriptures to prove it, too—familiar texts such as John 3:16 and Romans 6:23. But the point now is this, Have we recognized the *shift* element in the gospel? Have we recognized that what Jesus Christ cleansed by His blood, He claims? And that He claims not just a place in our lives, not even prominence in our lives, but preeminence?

Whether we are aware of it or not, we sing about it. "When I Survey the Wondrous Cross" is surely one of the church's favorite hymns. But as we sing through the verses of that hymn, where do they bring us? Right to Jabbok!

> Were the whole realm of nature mine,
>   That were a present far too small;
> Love so amazing, so divine,
>   Demands my soul, my life, my all.
>
> ISAAC WATTS

That, my friend, leads straight to the *second rest*. We know it best as surrender!

Do you know it? Have you taken that lonely walk from Bethel to Penuel and felt His touch upon the thigh of your soul? If so, you, too, have a limp, and special shoes to go with it. But it does not matter, now. You can even thank God for that limp, for with it has come a new name, a new power, and a new vision. You have declared your dependence!

5

The Glory of the Commonplace

WITH RARE EXCEPTION, I read Alexander Whyte's volumes, *Bible Characters*, with relish. But he disappointed me in something he said about my friend Isaac, favored son of Abraham, the patriarch. Here is a sample: "When I read Isaac's whole history over again. . .it becomes clear as a sunbeam to me that what envy was to Cain, and what wine was to Noah, and what lewdness was to Ham, and what wealth was to Lot, and what pride and impatience were to Sarah. . .venison and savory meat were to Isaac. . . .Old Isaac. . .is the father of all those men who make their god their belly."[1]

I have not so read the story of Isaac. Granted, his life was not to be compared to his father's or to his son's for that matter. As Griffith Thomas has said, Isaac "was the ordinary son of a great father, and the ordinary father of a great son." Which was true! But having acknowledged that fact, we hasten to add that there was a certain glory to that commonplace life which all of us who call ourselves Christians would do well to emulate. Here was a man "of the plain heroic breed, that loved heaven's silence more than fame."

The story is related very simply but fully in two verses in Genesis, chapter 26. Beginning at verse 24, we read, "The LORD appeared to him the same night, and said, I am the God of Abraham thy father: fear not, for I am with thee, and will bless thee, and multiply thy seed for my servant Abraham's sake. And he builded an altar there, and called upon the name of the LORD, and pitched his tent there: and there Isaac's servants digged a well" (vv. 24-25).

At once, our text introduces us to the revelation which Jehovah gave to this commoner, in which He confirmed His covenant with Abraham. It must have been a mighty moment for Isaac when God called on His servant. But in an equal sense, Isaac's response to that visit was no less remarkable in its own way. And it is to that response that we wish to confine this meditation, for here are the basic ingredients which give life meaning and purpose; they provide the pilgrim with shoes which are indeed iron and brass!

We read first that Isaac built an *altar*. In Old Testament times, altars were many and varied. Their importance may be gleaned from the fact that the term appears at least 433 times in our King James Version of the Bible. It appears first during the days of Noah, and suggests that one of the primary uses of the altar was for sacrifice. Isaac knew something about that from personal experience. In company with his beloved father, Abraham, he had made the long trek into the land of Moriah, and from there to the mount which God had appointed, to make a sacrifice of a burnt offering. All the ingredients for the sacrifice were accounted for. The wood was there. The fire was there. And Abraham carried the knife.

But it was at this point that Isaac remembered something—the lamb for the offering. This prompted the question which must have struck a dreadful blow into that father's heart, "Behold the fire and the wood: but where is the lamb for a burnt-offering?" (Gen 22:7). For the moment, the old man could only assure his son that God would see to that. But when they came to the place of which God had told him and Abraham had built his altar and placed the wood in order, he took his dearest treasure, whom he loved, and bound him and laid him on the altar prepared to take his life. In the mercy of God, the lad was spared, as we know; a ram was found and offered in Isaac's stead. But the lad never forgot that experience, nor the lesson it taught his tender heart. In a word, it was this: God's claim upon us comes *first*! It is a direct appeal to the vertical relationship, which should have priority in the life of the child of God.

This should not surprise us, who have the fuller light of

New Testament revelation. This was the persistent plea of
our Lord Jesus Christ in the days of His flesh. As He walked
the shores of Galilee and watched the multitudes of human
driftwood, He saw them collapse morally and spiritually
under the weight of the horizontal things of this life. It was in
such circumstances that He cried on one occasion, "Seek ye
first the kingdom of God, and his righteousness; and all these
things shall be added unto you" (Mt 6:33). What was He
trying to say to them? He was trying to tell them where to
find the key which opens the door behind which all the other
keys are kept. To His sensitive spirit, a spiritual philosophy
of life was not incidental but imperative. It led the list of
indispensables!

Here is a timely and necessary lesson for all of us who live
in a world where affluence oftentimes blinds us to the things
which abide! For too long, now, we have sown the winds of
materialism and secularism, until today we are reaping the
whirlwind, with its dangerous and deadly fallouts which
threaten the destruction of the souls of men with little more
than miserable muckrakes in their hands! We have time for
everything but eternity!

Thank God, then, for Isaac! Call him ordinary, if you
must. But that man has something to say to our generation.
His personal response to the revelation of Jehovah was right
and proper; it was his way of recognizing God's rightful
claim upon his life.

After the altar was in its place, Isaac pitched his *tent*. That
tent intrigues me; there must be something besides the skins
and stakes which formed its materials. May it not be that the
Spirit of God means to suggest in that tent a vivid display of
life as a pilgrimage? We know that the idea is inherent in all of
life, but that tent seems to give it visible expression.

I believe that in that modest dwelling, our friend was
openly confessing that he was a stranger here, on his way to
something better. How else are we to understand the biblical
commentary on this very thought, as set forth in Hebrews
11:9-10? There, the Holy Spirit tells us that "By faith he

[Abraham] sojourned in the land of promise, as in a strange country, dwelling in tabernacles [tents] with Isaac and Jacob, the heirs with him of the same promise: for he looked for a city which hath foundations, whose builder and maker is God." And a bit later in that same text we read, "[they] confessed that they were strangers and pilgrims on the earth" (v. 13).

Their confession was beautifully set forth in their tent. Full well they knew that they had "no continuing city" here! Thus they looked for a city that *had* foundations.

Do we see that our lot is cast with this dear man and his fathers? Have we forgotten the admonition which speaks on this wise, "Dearly beloved, I beseech you as strangers and pilgrims, abstain from fleshly lusts, which war against the soul" (1 Pe 2:11). You see, this world is not home for us who belong to Jesus Christ; we are just passing through! For that reason, we must not drive down our tent pegs so firmly as to suggest that we intend to stay here forever! As the aged apostle John reminds us, "The world passeth away, and the lust thereof: but he that doeth the will of God abideth for ever" (1 Jn 2:17).

Perhaps this story, which appeared years ago in *Readers Digest* and was written by Billy Rose, will put the issue in perspective.

There was once a fellow who, with his father, farmed a little piece of land. Several times a year they'd load up the ox-cart with vegetables and drive to the nearest city. Except for their name and the patch of ground, father and son had little in common. The old man believed in taking it easy. . .and the son was the go-getter type.

One morning, they loaded the cart, hitched up the ox and set out. The young fellow figured that if they kept going all day and night, they'd get to the market by next morning. He walked alongside the ox and kept prodding it with a stick.

"Take it easy," said the old man. "You'll last longer."

"If we get to the market ahead of the others," said his son, "we have a better chance of getting good prices."

The old man pulled his hat down over his eyes and went to sleep on the seat. Four miles and four hours down the road, they came to a little house. "Here's your uncle's place," said the father, waking up. "Let's stop in and say hello."

"We've lost an hour already," complained the go-getter.

"Then a few minutes more won't matter," said his father. "My brother and I live so close, yet we see each other so seldom."

The young man fidgeted while the two old gentlemen gossiped away an hour. On the move again, the father took his turn leading the ox. By and by, they came to a fork in the road. The old man directed the ox to the right. "The left is the shorter way," said the boy. "I know it," said the old man, "but this way is prettier."

"Have you no respect for time?" asked the impatient young man.

"I respect it very much," said the old fellow. "That's why I like to use it for looking at pretty things." The right-hand path led through woodland and wild flowers. The young man was so busy watching the sun sink he didn't notice how lovely the sunset was. Twilight found them in what looked like one big garden.

"Let's sleep here," said the old man.

"This is the last trip I take with you," snapped his son. "You're more interested in flowers than in making money."

"That's the nicest thing you've said in a long time," smiled the old fellow. A minute later he was asleep. A little before sunrise, the young man shook his father awake. They hitched up and went on. A mile and an hour away they came upon a farmer trying to pull his cart out of a ditch.

"Let's give him a hand," said the father.

"And lose more time?" exploded the son.

"Relax," said the old man. "You might be in a ditch some time yourself."

By the time the other cart was back on the road, it was almost eight o'clock. Suddenly a great flash of lightning split the sky. Then there was thunder. Beyond the hills, the heavens grew dark.

"Looks like a big rain in the city," said the old man.

"If we had been on time, we'd be sold out by now,"

grumbled his son.

"Take it easy," said the old gentlemen. "You'll last longer."

It wasn't until late in the afternoon that they got to the top of the hill overlooking the town. They looked down at it for a long time. Neither of them spoke. Finally the young man who had been in such a hurry said, "I see what you mean, father."

They turned their cart around and drove away from what had once been the city of Hiroshima.[2]

Such is the lesson of the tent.

But the end is not yet! Having built his altar and pitched his tent, Isaac had one more thing which needed attention: "And there," we read, "Isaac's servants digged a *well*" (Gen 26:25). It may not appear very important to us, but in Isaac's day, wells were one of the bare necessities of life. That motley crowd of families with their flocks, led by Moses to the border of the promised land, was acutely water conscious. So much so, in fact, that the digging of a well was an occasion for community rejoicing and singing. In Numbers we read, "Then sang Israel this song: Spring up, O well; sing ye unto it: The well, which the princes digged, Which the nobles of the people delved; With the sceptre, and with their staves" (Num 21:17, ASV).

What a blessing, then, that well of Isaac's must have been to him, his family, and the community.

But beyond that, we trace a spiritual lesson for our hearts. That well speaks of our horizontal concern for those all about us. And this is a matter which all true believers should consider, for it rounds out the full purpose for which God brought us to Himself. We were not converted to be introverted! *He* could not be hid, the Scripture tells us. Neither must we, for it is in this forum of our faith that we may exercise our maximum influence to a world of needy people.

My personal involvement with the students at Dallas Theological Seminary provides a fitting illustration of this truth. Each year, it falls to my lot to interview the entering class of seminarians. In the course of my interview, I invariably ask this question: What human influence brought you to this school? With almost unanimous response, they affirm what I already suspect—that it was *someone* who encouraged them to come to the seminary. A Dallas graduate or a friend of the seminary—these were the well diggers!

In retrospect, it was so in my own life. During those difficult days of the depression, when all thoughts of a college education were remote, insofar as I was concerned, it was a small Jewess in a high school Latin class who first challenged me to even consider college and then gave me the impetus to do something toward that end. Little did she know it then, but she dug the first strategic well in my academic life. Then it was another woman, a godly woman this time, who turned my steps from a secular college to Wheaton College. And it was there that the Spirit of God tapped me for the ministry. And finally, my coming to Dallas Seminary was the result of yet another well digger. This time a faithful pastor, sensing my dilemma regarding the right seminary for me, gave me the right word, "Son, if you want to go to a seminary and know how to wear your tails, go to _____, but if you want to know your Bible, go to Dallas."

I had my answer. The well was dug. I came to Dallas, never to regret it!

Such is the history of all of God's children. There have been well diggers who have crossed the trail of our lives and influenced us for God and His kingdom; not only individually but in the Church of God. Think how indebted we are to those giants of the faith who spawned great church movements or led the Church into new truth.

This is the thrilling challenge which comes to all of us.

There *is* glory to the commonplace, after all. Isaac was right in what he did and in the order in which he did it. First, the altar; then the tent; and finally, the well. Surely, if these things be in us and abound, they shall make us that we "shall neither be barren nor unfruitful in the knowledge [and service] of our Lord Jesus Christ" (2 Pe 1:8).

6
For the Time of Your Life

IN HIS BOOK *For the Living of These Days*, William M. Elliott, Jr., observes, "The reason why so many of us are overwrought, tense, distracted, and anxious is that we have never mastered the art of living one day at a time. Physically we do live a day at a time. We can't quite help ourselves. But mentally we live in all three tenses at once—past, present, and future. . . .And that will not work! 'The load of tomorrow, added to that of yesterday, carried today makes the strongest falter.'"[1]

Perhaps this helps us to understand why the Word of God lays such repeated emphasis upon the fact that man's time here on earth is measured in terms of *days*. Hear these witnesses: "Our days upon earth are a shadow" (Job 8:9); "Are thy days as the days of man?" Job inquires. "Are thy years as man's days?" (Job 10:5); "Man that is born of a woman is of few days" (Job 14:1).

No surprise, therefore, to find Moses praying, "So teach us to number our days, that we may apply our hearts unto wisdom" (Ps 90:12).

There are several ways of responding to that prayer. One is a bit novel, but nonetheless thought provoking. Someone has reduced the normal life to the length of one day, and used as his yardstick the hours from seven in the morning until eleven o'clock at night. With this guide, he produced the following statistics: at age twenty, it is 11:30 A.M.; at thirty, it is 2:00 P.M.; at forty, it is 4:00 P.M.; at fifty, it is 6:30 P.M.; at sixty, it is 8:45 P.M.

To press the question, what time is it for *you*?

But there is a biblical approach to this matter, which is considerably more stimulating and helpful. It is fivefold.

First, let me speak of the *daily code*. The dictionary defines the word *code* as "a systematic book of law." Not an inappropriate definition for the Bible. One of God's servants has described it as the "King's Highway Code." In any case, the important point is that there should be a daily appointment with this inspired revelation of God. The Bereans practiced this, for it was said of them, "They received the word with all readiness of mind, and searched the scriptures daily, whether those things were so" (Ac 17:11).

Much could be said in support of such a practice. For example, the Bible is *unique*. It provides the only complete unfolding of the plan of God for this planet Earth. It alone records God's dealings with His ancient people, the Jews. It alone provides a record of the beginning of the church of God. The Bible is also *effective*. It gives meaning to life. It is the chief way whereby God speaks to men. It has sustained mankind in the fiercest trials of our race. And finally, the Word of God is *timeless*. Its central message is never dated; it speaks equally to every generation.

William E. Gladstone, nineteenth-century British statesman and prime minister, bore his personal witness to the Bible when he said,

> This great spiritual library shows me how to meet and overcome life's temptations, sorrows and oppressions. It furnishes me techniques for the mastery of fear, anxiety and despair. The Word of God corrects my perspective, and saves me from being undone by the immediate. It gives me something which all of us need so much in these desperate days—the long view. It tells me in Emerson's words, "what the years and the centuries are saying as against the hours."[2]

Little wonder, then, that the ancient prophet Jeremiah left

this witness to the Word: "Thy words were found, and I did eat them; and thy word was unto me the joy and rejoicing of mine heart" (Jer 15:16).

The Psalter gives us several choice suggestions as to the best use of our days. Take this, for instance: "Lord, I have called daily upon thee, I have stretched out my hands unto thee" (Ps 88:9). What a lovely term with which to describe the *daily call*! Perhaps we have not thought of prayer in this simplistic form, but certainly the Bible encourages us so to think of it. Speaking for God, Asaph writes, "Offer unto God thanksgiving; and pay thy vows unto the most High; and call upon me in the day of trouble: I will deliver thee, and thou shalt glorify me" (Ps 50:14-15).

I believe, in essence, this idea of the daily call is so suggestive of prayer's nontechnical substance. Just call—as a child would call its mother; as a drowning man would call for help; as one might call the doctor in the deep of night, when sickness has stricken a loved one.

It is something anyone can do and ought to do. And the more simple the call, the better.

I recall Dr. Lewis Sperry Chafer's story in this connection. It seems that a certain minister was in the habit of profound prayers, oftentimes resorting to words beyond the ken of his simple flock. This went on week after week, to the dismay and frustration of the congregation. At last, a wee Scottish woman in the choir ventured to take the matter in hand. On a given Sunday, as the minister was waxing his most eloquently verbose, the little woman reached across the curtain separating the choir from the pulpit. Taking a firm grasp on the frock tail of the minister, she gave it a yank, and was heard to whisper, "Jes' call Him Fether, and ask 'im for somethin.' "

After all, that is what prayer is all about, is it not?

There is a third gem from the book of Psalms. I call this one the *daily chore*. Consider this as a good text: "So will I sing praise unto thy name for ever, that I may daily perform my vows" (Ps 61:8). The dictionary defines a chore as "a

small or odd job. " There is not anything overwhelming or
dramatic about the term or its definition; yet it carries its own
peculiar message to those of us who really value our days
here on earth.

In his devotional book, *Daily Readings*, W. E. Sangster,
relates the following story:

> Some years ago, in the midst of much toilsome work and not a
> few perplexities, I received a letter from a stranger. It was a
> lovely letter. It seemed to see right into my situation and,
> with almost uncanny discernment, to sense my need. . . .
> Though the letter required no answer. . .(my correspondent
> explained that he did not wish to add to my work) I sent a
> word of the warmest gratitude, and some months later we
> met. Let me tell you about this obscure disciple and some-
> thing of his secret service for our Lord. He is a shy man. It
> would be wrong to say that he has no gift in public speech, but
> he has a greater gift in writing. Years ago he went to God for
> guidance, asking how best he could serve the coming of the
> Kingdom, and it was revealed to him that a ministry awaited
> him in correspondence. . . .He accepted the commission. For
> years he has been fulfilling it. He does it with prayer and (as
> he believes) under guidance. The number of people he has
> encouraged must, by now, be immense. He writes to all kinds
> of folk—to friends, to acquaintances, to entire strangers; to
> the authors of books which have helped him; to people in
> public life who are carrying great responsibilities; to high and
> humble, known and unknown, rich and poor. He writes to
> sick people and speaks of his admiration for their courage.
> He lets the lonely know that he remembers them. He backs
> up those who are battling for social righteousness, especially
> when they are maligned. A letter of comfort from him has
> soothed a hundred broken hearts. . . .He is a quietly happy
> man; happy with the happiness of those who found their
> work. . .and do it. He offers no advice in his letters and makes
> it plain that he expects no reply. He *specializes in apprecia-
> tion* [italics mine]. There are enough critics, he believes,
> eager to tell a man where he is wrong. . . .So often has he been
> assured of the *timeliness* of his letter's arrival that he cannot
> possibly doubt that he is working with Another.[3]

For whatever encouragement it may be to others, I must record that the Spirit of God used this simple story in my own life, and to this day, I find the greatest satisfaction in writing a letter to someone!

Obviously, there are other chores, but this is a good one, and a simple way to start.

The end is not yet! To the daily code, the daily call, and the daily chore, we must add a fourth—the *daily cross*. *We* did not add it, however; it was His idea. Remember, He said to His disciples after the feeding of the five thousand, "If any man will come after me, let him deny himself, and take up his cross daily, and follow me" (Lk 9:23). It is no secret that with many of us, the usual interpretation is related to some physical or mental weakness. "It's my cross, and I must bear it," we often hear people say. While recognizing the nagging reality of such things in our bodies, at the same time I do not believe that this was our Lord's meaning of the word *cross*. Borrowing a thought from A. W. Tozer, we must recognize that the cross was the symbol of death; it stood for the abrupt, violent end of a human being. The man in Roman times who took up his cross and started down the road had already said good-bye to his friends. He was not coming back. He was not going out to have his life redirected; he was going out to have it ended! The cross made no compromise, modified nothing, spared nothing; it slew all of the man, completely and for good. It did not try to keep on good terms with its victim. It struck swift and hard, and when it had finished its work, the man was no more.

Does this offend us? It did not offend the apostle, for he wrote to the church at Galatia, "But God forbid that I should glory, save in the cross of our Lord Jesus Christ, by whom the world is crucified unto me, and I unto the world" (Gal 6:14).

All these things make Elizabeth Clephane's hymn more demanding, especially that verse:

> I take, O cross, thy shadow
> For my abiding place;

> I ask no other sunshine than
> The sunshine of His face;
> Content to let the world go by,
> To know no gain nor loss,
> My sinful self my only shame,
> My glory all the cross.

Then cometh the end! But it is a good end, and a needful one, for it is often the neglected part of our daily habit. I speak now of the *daily care*. We find a sample of it in the Hebrew epistle, "But exhort one another daily, while it is called To day" (Heb 3:13). Weymouth translates the word "exhort" with the more contemporary term *encourage*. The net result is the same; it means caring for the perishing and all the injured on society's roadside, especially those of the household of faith.

Of such was the house of Stephanas. The apostle Paul could write of them, "They have addicted themselves to the ministry of the saints" (1 Co 16:15). *There* is a legitimate form of addiction, to which all of us may aspire. If we really believe this, let us join Fanny Crosby as she sings what only faith can see through blinded eyes:

> Down in the Human heart,
> Crushed by the tempter,
> Feelings lie buried that grace can restore;
> Touched by a loving heart,
> Wakened by kindness,
> Chords that were broken will vibrate once more.

And so, there is a day's work. It includes just five "day-tight compartments": the daily code, the daily call, the daily chore, the daily cross, and the daily care. But surely, if these things be in us and abound, they shall make us that we shall neither be barren nor unfruitful in the knowledge and service of the King.

7
A Parable on Christian Trees

A CURSORY READING of the New Testament reveals the abundance and value of the parabolic method of teaching. While this use of parables was a unique and at the same time a major teaching device of our Lord, for, "Without a parable spake he not unto them" (Mt 13:34), He did not invent this method of teaching. Parables were popular among the peoples of the East. Dr. S. D. Salmond, in his handbook, *The Parables of Our Lord*, reminds us in the paragraph entitled "The Charm of Figurative Speech" that speech of this kind had a "special attraction for the peoples of the East, with whom the imagination was quicker and more active than the logical faculty. The great family of nations known as the Semitic, to which the Hebrews, together with the Arabs, the Syrians, the Babylonians, and other remarkable races belong, has shown a particular genius and liking for it."[1]

With this word of background, we are not surprised to discover that the parable found its way into the teaching of the Old Testament. It appears initially in the little-known book of Judges. And, in harmony with our basic intention in this series, I believe this parable shows both the delights and the dangers along the highway to the Celestial City, and how to win through to victory in the face of them.

Judges, chapter 9 is our text, but it draws its life from the chapter which precedes it. There we are exposed to the closing days of one of Israel's truly great soldier-judges, Gideon, the son of Joash. For the greater part of his noble life, he was both famous and faithful to his God-given task. But alas! Gideon lived a little too long! The very man who in his earlier days distinguished himself as one of the nation's great leaders, experienced a strange decline in his loyalty to Jehovah, and in the end "encouraged idol-worship, and himself fell under its carnal fascinations, until the land was riddled through and through, like a moth-fretted garment, with idolatrous practices and moral degradation." Thus wrote Stuart Holden in *Some Old Testament Parables*.

It is not surprising, therefore, to come upon the sad and tragic story which we find in our text. Disobedience bears its own fruit; Gideon bore Abimelech. It happened on this wise. Following the death of Gideon, referred to in our text as Jerubbaal (a name given to him by his father after he had cast down the altar of Baal), the restraint and example of his powerful personality were gone. It was not surprising, therefore, that anarchy and civil war should invade the kingdom, and some unscrupulous chap should seize the moment for personal advantage. Abimelech, Gideon's own flesh and blood, was that kind of a man. He took advantage of the unsettled state of the kingdom, murdered all of his brothers save young Jotham, and claimed the crown which his father had previously refused. That he succeeded in his headstrong mission Scripture leaves no doubt, for we read, "And all the men of Shechem gathered together, and all the house of Millo, and went, and made Abimelech king, by the plain of the pillar that was in Shechem" (Judg 9:6).

That much is history.

It is just here that young Jotham, Abimelech's brother who had somehow evaded his brother's murderous escapade, appears from nowhere and takes his stand on the top of mount Gerizim to address his parable to the sons of Shechem and to every generation of the sons of men since. In meditating on the parable, two things seem clear: there is an obvious, local, temporary application as it relates to Abimelech; but secondly, there is a larger and more permanent meaning which is designed to address the hearts of all who have ears to hear.

And so, for the moment, we consider Abimelech.

It is not often that the Bible employs sarcasm, but when it does, it bites like acid! When it chooses to cover a man with ignominy, it literally buries him! I think Jotham's parable does just that. In his parable, the young brother related an account of the trees meeting together for the purpose of choosing a king over them.

In the order of our text, the trees approached the olive tree, the fig tree, and the vine. To each, the proposition is offered, "Reign thou over us." But to their dismay, the trees which they had suspected might be tempted to respond to such an offer refused, and their grounds for doing so were clear. Said the olive tree, "Should I leave my fatness, wherewith by me they honour God and man, and go to be promoted over the trees?" (v. 9). Replied the fig tree to the same request, "Should I forsake my sweetness, and my good fruit, and go to be promoted over the trees?" (v. 11). And finally, the lowly vine made its own retort, "Should I leave my wine, which cheereth God and man, and go to be promoted over the trees?" (v. 13).

It was evident that the Committee for the Election of a King had failed completely. They learned the hard way that they were dealing with the company of the committed!

But the Committee was not to be denied. As a last resort, they turned to the bramble with the same request, "Come thou, and reign over us!" To their surprise—and delight no doubt—the bramble replied immediately but severely, "If in truth ye anoint me king over you, then come and put your trust in my shadow; and if not, let fire come out of the bramble, and devour the cedars of Lebanon" (v. 15).

I am not a psychologist. But if I were, I should diagnose this as a plain case of delusions of grandeur! Who ever heard of a bramble casting a shadow? When did anyone ever see a bramble dictate its own direction? Yet, here it is, laying down the terms upon which it will consent to rule: "Bow or burn! I will either rule you, or ruin you!"

Keeping within the limits of the local application to which reference was made earlier, I think we can see that this was

Jotham's way of exposing the unprincipled and unreasonable demand of Abimelech. But further, "It warned these Shechemites of the character of Abimelech: that he is nothing more than a mean and worthless and flesh-tearing thorn-bush, whose end is to be burned, that he will do them no good if they yield to his bluster, that he will involve them in his own destruction."[2] This seems to be the clear meaning of Jotham's words in verses 19 and 20 of our text. There he says, "If ye then have dealt truly and sincerely with Jerubbaal and with his house this day, then rejoice ye in Abimelech, and let him also rejoice in you: But if not, let fire come out from Abimelech, and devour the men of Shechem and from the house of Millo, and devour Abimelech." In point of fact, this is precisely what happened, as the closing verses of the chapter relate. It is a solemn requiem indeed!

But now for the wider and more permanent application of this parable.

Consider, first of all, the lessons to be gleaned from the fruit trees. There was the matter of their variety. They were all different. There were the olive, the fig, and the vine. Then, there was the matter of their diversity of function —fatness in the case of the olive; sweetness from the fig; and wine to cheer the heart of God and man from the lowly vine. Lastly, and perhaps most remarkably, there was the matter of their tenacity in regard to their natural endowment. They would not desert their individual functions, even for the questionable honor of being king of the trees!

I suspect a question just here. Pray tell, how does this relate to a twentieth-century Christian? We are not trees! But you see, we really are! This is the thrilling figure employed by the psalmist when he describes the happy man. What is he like? A tree "planted by the rivers of water, that bringeth forth his fruit in his season; his leaf also shall not wither; and whatsoever he doeth shall prosper" (Ps 1:3). And what shall we say of the repetitious references to believers as trees, especially in the teaching of our Lord in the gospels?

So we are trees of the Lord's own planting, and in that spiritual frame, we may properly expect to find spiritual applications from those fruit trees. We may speak of variety in the Lord's spiritual vineyard, as well as diversity of function. These things come through loud and clear from such New Testament passages as Romans 12:3-8; 1 Corinthians 12:4-11; and Ephesians 4:7-16. They merit our careful reading and relating to every believer's life. And what about the matter of tenacity? Have we forgotten John 15:16? There, you recall, the Saviour addressed Himself to His disciples in these words, "Ye have not chosen me, but I have chosen you, and ordained you, that ye should go and bring forth fruit, and that your fruit should *remain*." To what end have we been gifted as individual believers? That our fruit might abide!

This is both the privilege and peril of the gift endowed upon us by the Spirit of God. The privilege: that our gift might remain, or be "lasting," as J. B. Phillips translates it. Nothing in the kingdom of grace is more refreshing than a believer who is exercising his gift of ministry, administration, teaching, singing, praying, or whatever, for the profit of the body of believers. And what of the peril? Ah, there is the grief to the heart of any true shepherd of the flock—to see one of his sheep yield to the enticements of the world, the flesh, or the devil and thereby dissipate the exercise of his gift. It is just here that many churches find themselves fulfilling only part-time their holy calling; the "trees" are busy crowning kings.

But now we must turn our attention to the more serious warning of the bramble. It may come to us as a new thought, but we need to think about it, for it is an ever present danger: there are bramble believers! Strange as it may seem, there are those "making their personal advancement the one thing in life, scheming and plotting, blustering and sneaking, trampling on others, and bloating themselves with vain ambition, and creating their own false and poisonous inspirations by their subtle self-appreciation—all to secure some advantage for themselves."[3]

Stuart Holden dares to raise the question in his own words:

> Is that warning superfluous amongst us? Is it not because the brambles are so numerous, and so pathetically unconscious that they are "spotted" as brambles by those whom they want to impress; because there are so many climbers, pushers, vulgarians, even in Christian circles, in whose hearts there is no real reverence for God or man—but only for themselves—that there is so much dispeace and lovelessness and so little real fellowship amongst Christian groups? Unscrupulous intention, jealousy, greed of gain, lust for prominence, forwardness, the levity of empty self-conceit —these are the things that dishonour the Holy Name by which we are called. And how common they are! There is a shaft of ironic wit in the attention the parable calls to the silly vanity of the bramble. What a fool it unwittingly shows itself to be, in avidly seizing the kingship of the trees, for which office it has not the slightest fitness. . . .What fools we Christians make of ourselves when we turn from the simple ways of Jesus Christ to the devious ways of selfishness! And how inevitably we advertise our folly![4]

Does this seem an overstatement of the truth? Let us answer that question by turning from the language of men to the lives of men. There is a revealing portrayal of this whole parable in 3 John. In verse 9, the aged apostle John writes his friend Gaius thusly: "I wrote unto the church: but Diotrephes, who loveth to have the preeminence among them, receiveth us not."

Of what speakest the apostle? Whose image is this? Why, it is the bramble, in flesh and blood! And see further how he describes this man's activities in the church: "I. . .remember his deeds which he doeth, prating against us with malicious words: and not content therewith, neither doth he himself receive the brethren, and forbiddeth them that would, and casteth them out of the church" (v. 10). Think of it!

It is not welcome news, but it is necessary; Diotrephes' disease has not yet been eliminated from the body of Christians.

But now look again at the little letter that John wrote, and see the lovely portrait he draws in verse 12. "Demetrius hath good report of all men, and of the truth itself: yea, and we also bear record; and ye know that our record is true."

The names are so much alike—Diotrephes, Demetrius. But how different their natures! The one was a blight in the church; the other a blessing.

Whether we have been aware of it or not, the Holy Spirit has been taking our photograph in this meditation. And in examining the proofs, we discover that we are either in one company or the other. We are either in the company of the noble, self-denying fruit trees (of which Demetrius is such a splendid specimen), bearing love's fruit and blessing hearts around us; or we belong to that ignoble, strutting order of the bramble bush (of which Diotrephes is such a sad specimen), spreading self's fire and blighting all we touch. It is either fruit or fire.

The question lingers and waits for our answer. To which company do we belong?

8
When Doing Your Thing
May Not Be Christian

DEEPLY IMPRESSED with the ministry of John Fawcett
when he preached at Carter's Lane Church, London, the
people of that parish called him to succeed their recently
deceased pastor, Dr. John Gill. Fawcett felt that he ought to
accept the invitation, so he resigned his church at Hebdon
Hill and subsequently preached his farewell sermon to his
little flock.

In due time, the packing was completed, and the pastor
and his family were prepared to leave. On the day of their
departure, the congregation gathered around their beloved
shepherd and his family, entreating them to reconsider and
remain with them.

So urgent were their entreaties that the parson's wife
turned to her husband and cried, "'Oh, John, John, I cannot
bear this! I know not how to go!' 'Nor I, either,' said the
good man. 'Nor will we go; unload the wagons, and put
everything in the place where it was before!'"[1]

To commemorate that touching scene, John Fawcett gave
verbal expression to his deep feeling about it in words familiar to every congregation. He wrote,

> Blest be the tie that binds
> Our hearts in Christian love;
> The fellowship of kindred minds
> Is like to that above.

Those of us who have tasted that fellowship in the bonds

55

of the Christian gospel have been privileged among men; the world does not have its equal. However, where that privilege is experienced and enjoyed, there lurks a subtle peril, the peril of the little foxes of peripheral differences which may invade the family of God. By and large, the differences are not doctrinal as they relate to the basic tenets of our faith but rather concern middle matters, that is, those areas in Christian life and practice where equally sincere believers may have honest differences of opinion. It is here that the blessed tie may be blasted and fellowship broken.

It should be stated at this point that these differences in doubtful things may be perfectly natural when we take into account the heterogeneity of any church fellowship—a heterogeneity born out of national, cultural, and even spiritual distinctives. These are the things which can spawn misunderstanding and, if not dealt with in the light of Scripture, can disrupt or even destroy the finest fellowship of Christians. Here are some shoes which may wear thin if we are not careful.

This raises the question; Has the Holy Spirit anticipated this hazard? Is there specific biblical instruction which speaks to this sensitive area of our life together? There is! And we can thank God for it, for if it is received and obeyed, it can forestall many a division among the saints of God. The text in question is Romans, chapter 14, as well as the first 7 verses of the following chapter. The entire section belongs together; there is no inspired break. It is here, more than anywhere else in the Bible, that we find principles which are designed to promote and preserve our life together. Mark it well; these are *principles*, not rules. Keeping this before us throughout this meditation will save us from gravitating toward legalism. The inspired instruction on this important subject is cast in the mold of grace, actuated by love, not law! The appeal in every case is "Let it be so!" not "Thou shalt!"

This brings us, then, to the first authoritative word. The fourteenth chapter of Romans opens in what could be a life-and-death struggle: "Him that is weak in the faith receive ye, but not to doubtful disputations." We must be careful, here, that we do not read into Paul's exhortation a word which is not there. He is not talking about a wicked man but a weak brother! The recognition of this fact will spare us at once from making the mistake that some believers make in their dealings with their brethren. This brother may be weak, that is, recently converted or immature through lack of proper teaching. But whatever the cause, he is to be received, for our fellowship in Christ is based upon *life*, not *light*! It is not how much one knows; it is who one knows! When that matter is settled in our own hearts, the weak brother is to be received without passing judgment on his foibles, scruples, or immature opinions and actions. As a dear saint of God once said in my hearing, "We are not here to split hairs, but to notify heirs!"

Now, in order to give substance to this delicate problem, Paul cites two very pertinent illustrations taken from everyday life. In verse 2, he speaks of the diet question: "One believeth that he may eat all things: another, who is weak, eateth herbs." Then, in verse 5, he touches upon the day question: "One man esteemeth one day above another: another esteemeth every day alike." Here they are, drawn up in battle array! Here is sufficient ammunition to blow apart the best of churches; and mind you, they are but two controversies among many.

What is the answer? If the brother will not bend to my way, should I break off fellowship with him? Some have done so. Or leave the church and go elsewhere? Some have done that, also. Or worse still, precipitate a split in the church? The very idea seems impossible! But alas, it has happened.

In the September 22, 1972 issue of *Life*, an article was published telling of a church where sharp differences had arisen over the attire of the minister's daughter at athletic events where she participated as a cheerleader. So divisive was the issue that the pastor was finally obliged to resign his church,

and official and congregational ties were severed which may
never be healed this side of the judgment seat of Christ.
Surely this cannot be God's way of settling our differences in these middle matters; there must be a better way.

Paul provides us with the inspired formula at the end of
verse 5. "Let every man be fully persuaded in his own
mind." The first principle which should control us in such
matters is *conviction*. Every believer should have his own
reasoned—and reasonable—convictions regarding these
doubtful things, regulate his own conduct by them, and at the
same time grant his brother the same privilege. That is where
that little word *let* comes in. The convictions I hold must be
two-directional, or the results may be devastating!

Over my years of ministry, I have witnessed in my own
life and in the lives of others the serious spiritual damage
which can be inflicted upon God's dear children where this
precept has been ignored or violated. It was that surgeon-
shepherd of Johns Hopkins, Dr. Howard Kelly, who said in
my hearing, "We may judge correctly, but we have never
judged righteously until we have also heard the other side."
Which brings us to another principle.

Beginning at verse 6 of our text, the apostle writes in
another vein. "He that regardeth the day, regardeth it unto
the Lord; and he that regardeth not the day, to the Lord he
doth not regard it. He that eateth, eateth to the Lord, for he
giveth God thanks; and he that eateth not, to the Lord he
eateth not, and giveth God thanks. For to this end Christ
both died and rose, and revived, that he might be Lord both
of the dead and the living" (Ro 14:6, 9).

Will you observe the repetition in these verses? It is ger-
mane to what should monitor our convictions. It is the word
"Lord." It suggests what we sometimes forget in these critical areas of conduct—that both the meat eater and the vegetarian stand related and responsible to Jesus Christ as *Lord*!
It has been well said, "The meat eater who says grace over
his steak and gives God glory is not different from the
vegetarian who asks a blessing over his salad."

Where the lordship of Christ presides, there must be *consideration* of one another in these middle matters. That is the second principle which should govern in "doing our thing." The basis for it appears in verse 13: "Let us not therefore judge one another any more: but judge this rather, that no man put a stumblingblock or an occasion to fall in his brother's way." You see, it is one thing to have personal convictions about doubtful things; it is something else—and something *more*—to be considerate of your brother's convictions.

Perhaps a page from personal experience will help here. In the early days of one of my pastorates, I found my lot cast among a group of believers with very strong convictions about certain peripheral matters, including eating in a public restaurant on Sunday. Before coming to that assembly, this matter had not been a problem with me; indeed, I had never even considered it a problem.

One Sunday evening, on my way to the service, I stopped off at the hospital to visit several patients and then stopped in at a diner for a quick snack. It happened that the place was filled with a cacophony of music, which hardly prepared me for the message. During the course of my sermon, I mentioned the incident in passing, little realizing that my own congregation as well as the radio audience in that metropolitan area had other thoughts about such a thing.

When I returned home that night after the service, I was scarcely in the house before the telephone rang, and a rough voice at the other end said, "Brother, I vant to ask you something. If you had died in dat diner tonight, where would you haf gone?"

Without hesitation, I replied, "Why, to heaven, my friend."

"Nothing of it, you would have gone straight to hell!"

This was a new invasion of my life and ministry, and for the moment I found my heart resenting it. The matter of eating in a restaurant or diner on Sunday was not all that important to me! But that was hardly the issue at this point.

The issue was this: Was I willing to be considerate of a weak brother (I trusted he was a brother) to the point of refraining from doing what I wanted to do? Indeed, I saw then that my responsibility involved not only this unknown caller, but it included my congregation as well, for there were many in it who shared that conviction! If I was to be the Lord's servant to these people, then I had to be willing to forgo something which to me was neither sinful nor harmful.

To support me in this struggle, I turned once again to our text, and I found these words from the apostle:

> I know, and am persuaded by the Lord Jesus, that there is nothing unclean of itself: but to him that esteemeth any thing to be unclean, to him it is unclean. But if thy brother be grieved with thy meat, now walkest thou not charitably. Destroy not him with thy meat, for whom Christ died. Let not then your good be evil spoken of: for the kingdom of God is not meat and drink; but righteousness, and peace, and joy in the Holy Ghost. For he that in these things serveth Christ is acceptable to God, and approved of men (Ro 14:14-18).

To this grand champion of grace, distinctions in matters of diet were gone; distinctions in matters of days were gone! With author William R. Newell, Paul would declare, "There is no place for religious fussing." All the same, however, Paul makes it clear that in this troublesome area of middle matters, what may be *allowable* for me—and I want to assert my freedom—may be *anathema* to my brother. And in such cases, his weak conscience must be considered, lest I wound him and weaken my own testimony. To emphasize the offense in such cases, Paul states in another place, concerning this selfsame truth, "When ye sin so against the brethren, and wound their weak conscience, ye sin against Christ" (1 Co 8:12).

That settled the matter for me, and it was not a problem during the balance of my ministry in that church. I had my convictions about doubtful things, but they were tempered now with consideration of others. Questions about habits of

life, amusements, and similar matters over which we may
have had honest differences of opinion were not dictated
now by a list of taboos, but by the law of love! It was love
that decided, and in that spirit I found my heart consenting to
the apostle's word of finality in such things, "Wherefore, if
meat make my brother to offend, I will eat no flesh while the
world standeth, lest I make my brother to offend" (1 Co
8:13).

Once we have executed that hurdle, we are ready for
Paul's third principle which should control our relationships
in regard to middle matters. In Romans 14:19, he writes,
"Let us therefore follow after the things which make for
peace, and things wherewith one may edify another."

Quite plainly, this is neither conviction nor consideration.
It is a call to higher ground, that of *contribution* to my weak
brother. The idea is inherent in that word "edify" and suggests building up, which is precisely what Paul tells us in
another place *love* does! Knowledge blows up; love builds
up! Now we are ready for the opening words of the fifteenth
chapter of Romans, for it is at this point that the apostle
addresses himself directly to what he calls the "strong"
believer and challenges him in this matter of edification of
the weaker brother.

But who is this "strong" believer? In terms of Scripture,
he is one who is mature in his knowledge of the things of
God. More than that, he is also mature in the application of
that knowledge in his life and conduct. It is to that man that
Paul now addresses himself in our text. "We then that are
strong ought to bear the infirmities of the weak, and not to
please ourselves. Let every one of us please his neighbour
for his good to edification (Ro 15:1-2).

It is unfortunate that the word *please* has been soiled by
ignoble use. The thought of the apostle is not the fawning or
flattering of a brother but the sincere desire to build up his
weak character. This will mean forbearing—bearing *with*,
not *down* upon—our brother's foibles. It will mean, as
Bonhoeffer pointed out, tolerating "his weaknesses and od-

dities, which are such a trial to our patience, everything that produces frictions, conflicts, and collisions among us."

Make no mistake about it, such a spirit does not come without some personal soul-searching. Dying to our righteous selves is most difficult! But in it all, difficult though it may be, there is the lovely example of our Lord Himself, who "pleased not himself; but, as it is written, The reproaches of them that reproached thee fell on me" (Ro 15:3). There is also the expectation that through our obedience to the exhortations of Scripture in these things, the Spirit of God may use us to contribute to our weaker brother's ultimate growth in grace, and we may see him come into the liberty which is ours in Jesus Christ.

I should be derelict to my experience if I failed to record that in the passing of years in the ministry, I have witnessed many young and immature in the faith, strapped and straddled with various forms of legalism and taboos, delivered into the sphere of righteousness, peace, and joy in the Holy Spirit. And the sight of these things has quickened my pace in the work and caused me to pray more fervently, "Lord, make me an instrument of Thy peace."

This brings us to the concluding principle. Romans 15:7 says, "Wherefore receive ye one another, as Christ also received us to the glory of God." There is *communion*. There is Christian fellowship which truly binds our hearts in Christian love. There is the one, inevitable hallmark of our faith!

Bishop Handley Moule is right when he says,

> How many a Church controversy, now as then, would die of inanition, leaving room for a living truth, if the disputants could only *gravitate* to their always most beloved theme, to the praises and glories of their redeeming Lord Himself! It is at His feet, and in His arms, that we best understand both His truth, and the thoughts, rightful or mistaken, of our brethren. . . .Let us "stand back and look at the picture." Here— conveyed in this strong petition—is St. Paul's idea of the true Christian's true life, and the true life of the true Church.[2]

9
Taken from an Eagle's Nest

THE CHURCH had had a long and honored ministry. The shepherd who had so recently left his flock behind to accept another pastorate had done an outstanding work—so much so, that it had precipitated a problem. What would the church do now? Who could ever replace the pastor? These were some of the questions which were being asked by that anxious congregation.

It was into that delicate situation that I was called, not as a possible successor to the pastor, whom I knew well, but to somehow heal the wound which his leaving had brought about. As I sat watching the service unfold and noticing particularly the expressions on the faces of that flock, my heart went out to them, for I knew what they were thinking and how they were feeling on this first Sunday without that familiar face in the pulpit. I saw the situation not only for what it was there—saints in shock—but also as representative of what happens in so many churches across the land when faithful men are called away, and the church is bereft of its shepherd. Nor was I unmindful of the additional fact that what I was witnessing in bulk was equally true of individual believers when the nest has been disturbed. Surely, there must be some word from the Lord for these dear people and the church of God everywhere! I searched for the shoe that would fit those feet!

It was then and there that the Spirit of God directed my thoughts to a timely word in the closing message of Moses, the man of God. The word was in his song in chapter 32 of Deuteronomy. There, certainly, we have one of the most comprehensive descriptions of God's dealings with His ancient people. For that particular occasion, my attention was directed to these words from the old patriarch: "For the LORD's portion is his people; Jacob is the lot of his inheritance. He found him in a desert land, and in the waste howling wilderness; he led him about, he instructed him, he kept him as the apple of his eye. As an eagle stirreth up her nest, fluttereth over her young, spreadeth abroad her wings, taketh them, beareth them on her wings: so the LORD alone did lead him" (Deu 32:9-12).

No man could sing that song better than Moses. He had spent eighty of his one-hundred-and-twenty years walking with God; he should have known something about Him and His ways with the children of men. As the ancient servant of God looked back upon all of life's days and ways, he saw an analogy between the ways of an eagle with her young and Jehovah with His people. And to his mind, the analogy was most appropriate just then, for his people were about to desert their roving life and settle down in a new and strange land. But more, they were about to lose their old leader and follow another, the youthful Joshua.

It was just there that the analogy came to life: "As an eagle. . .so the LORD." And it was just there, that morning, that I tried to share my heart and mind with a wounded, unsure flock of sheep. As I thought upon the analogy, four things seemed to clamor for utterance.

To begin with, as an eagle *builds*. For obvious reasons, we must begin there. An eagle's nest, called an aerie by ornithologists, is a remarkable wonder of nature. It is by no means a common sight, but where one has been found, either atop a very tall tree or balanced on some precipitous ledge, it reveals a huge, bulky gathering of branches, sticks, and all manner of material piled upon pile and weighing sometimes as much as a ton! To see one, then, is to see something extraordinary. The eagle builds!

So does God! Even before Moses sang about it, Abraham knew it was so, for we read, "He looked for a city which hath foundations, whose *builder* and maker is God" (Heb 11:10). His longing was not in vain, for we read in another place, "For he hath prepared for them a city" (Heb 11:16). God gave further confirmation of this in the witness of Jesus Christ, who said, "I will *build* my church; and the gates of hell shall not prevail against it" (Mt 16:18). It was with that promise before him that the apostle Paul could say to the Corinthian church, "Ye are God's *building*" (1 Co 3:9).

As an eagle builds, then, so does God!

The song of Moses had a second verse. "As an eagle stirreth up her nest." So ran the lyrics. Now we are coming closer to the problem which faced my friends, for as an eagle *breaks*, so does God!

The eagle's nest is not for always. Once the eggs are deposited in the nest, there is an incubation period of at least one month followed by the hatching and normal growth of the eaglets, extending over an additional eight to eleven weeks. It takes time, for eagles are large birds. But when the time has expired, the parent birds have an eagle's job to do; they must stir up the nest, and they do so with abandon! The softer materials are beaked from the inner part of the nest, leaving only the jagged, rough sticks and branches. Very soon, the young get the message and begin to stir. All of this, of course, is part of the program of nature; the parents want their bairns to fly! But they know that they must be prodded to do so!

"As an eagle," sang Moses, "so the LORD." God breaks up the nest of His fledgings. This is an aspect of divine dealing about which we know little and wish we did not have to know anything. It is the principle of divine disturbance. God is the *author* of change, not the antagonist. The truth is illustrated again and again in Scripture, but never more vividly than in Jeremiah's prophecy. There it is written, "Moab hath been at ease from his youth, and he hath settled on his lees, and hath not been emptied from vessel to vessel, neither hath he gone into captivity: therefore his taste remained in him, and his scent is not changed. Therefore, behold, the days come, saith the LORD, that I will send unto him wanderers, that shall cause him to wander, and shall empty his vessels, and break their bottles" (Jer 48:11-12).

Alas! What had happened in that fine church was what happens in every eagle's nest; the comfort of a settled ministry had been disturbed, and the congregation was restless, afraid they might have to take to their wings! But they need not have feared, for this brings us to another remarkable provision of the eagle for its young, and it constitutes the third verse of the song of God's servant, Moses. "As an eagle. . .fluttereth over her young, spreadeth abroad her wings."

The eagle builds. The eagle breaks. But the eagle also *broods*!

What a fascinating study to observe the parent birds at this point in the life cycle of their little family. Again and again, the old birds flutter over the nest to show the young birds how to fly. There is an interesting point just here: no eaglet learns to fly by watching another eaglet!

God also broods over His little flock of fledgings. This comes through so very clearly in His relationship with Israel, particularly in the guiding cloud mentioned in Numbers 9:15-23. There we are told, in part, that on the day the tabernacle was reared up, the cloud covered the tabernacle. And so it was always; the cloud covered it by day, and the appearance of fire was upon it by night. When the cloud tarried, the people tarried; when the cloud moved, the people moved. Everything was determined by that supernatural cloud which brooded over the people of God. C. H. Mackintosh wrote,

> What a spectacle! There were those millions of people moving along without any knowledge of the route which they were to travel, as wholly dependent upon God for guidance as for food and all beside; a thoroughly helpless pilgrim host. They could form no plans for the morrow. When encamped, they knew not when they were to march, and

when on the march, they knew not when or where they were
to halt. Theirs was a life of daily and hourly dependence. . . .
Their movements were controlled by the wheels of
Jehovah's chariot.[1]

Thus it was with Israel, and thus it should be with us.

This brooding ministry of God is never more available
than when a church is without a visible shepherd. It is then
that God reminds the sensitive hearts that He is still there.

William L. Pettingill shared an incident with me which
relates to this matter. He was to minister in a church in
Richmond, Virginia. The church had just lost its honored
minister, and the sheep were looking for help. But they were
a distressed flock; their faces and actions showed it. As
God's servant came into their midst to minister, he sensed
their distress, and in his typical, incisive manner, he turned
to the men of the board and remarked, "Brethren, cheer up!
God isn't dead; He isn't even sick!" They got the message
and hopefully remembered the cloud! It had been there all
the time, brooding over them.

But now we must come to the main event, for which all the
other events are preliminary. This is the day when the young
must sally forth for their solo flight. William M. J. Long, in
his book *Fowls of the Air*, relates a firsthand account of what
happens at this point.

One day when I came to the little thicket on the cliff, I found
that one eagle was gone. The other stood on the edge of the
nest. Presently the mother eagle came swiftly up the valley,
and there was food in her talons. She came to the edge of the
nest, hovered over it for a moment, then went slowly down to
the valley, taking the food with her, telling the little one in her
own way to come and he could have it. But he was afraid. In a
little while she came back again, this time without food, and
tried every way to induce the little one to leave the nest. She
succeeded at last, when with a desperate effort he sprang
upward and flapped to the ledge above; then after surveying
the world gravely from his new place, he flapped back to the
nest. Suddenly, as if discouraged, she rose well above him. I

held my breath for I knew what was coming. The little fellow stood on the edge of the nest, looking down at the plunge which he dared not take. There was a sharp cry from behind, which made him alert, tense as a watch-spring. The next instant the mother eagle had swooped, striking the nest at his feet, sending his support of twigs and himself with them into the air together. He was aloft now, and flapped lustily for life. Over him, under him, beside him hovered the mother on tireless wings, calling softly that she was there. But the awful fear of the depths and the lance tops of spruces was upon the little one; his flapping grew more wild: he fell faster and faster. Suddenly—more in fright, it seemed to me, than because he had spent his strength—he lost his balance and tipped head downward in the air. Then like a flash the old mother eagle shot under him. He righted himself, rested an instant, found his head; then she dropped like a shot from under him, leaving him to come down on his own wings. It was all the work of an instant before I lost them among the trees far below. And when I found them again with my glasses, the eaglet was in the top of a great pine, and the mother was feeding him.

Such a thrilling experience does not come to many, but William Long saw it all, and his record is true to an eagle's ways.

God is like an eagle; He builds; He breaks; He broods; but He also *bears*! "As an eagle. . .taketh them, beareth them on her wings. . .so the Lord."

It was my delicate but delightful task to remind the saints on that Sunday morning that when the church's sky is leaden gray and the clouds come rolling up, black over blue, and days of deep depression and anxiety overwhelm because the pastor has gone; when the church thinks that things can never possibly be the same again; when it seems that the bottom has fallen out of everything, and you are about to drop down, down, down; then to realize that underneath, unfailing and ever sustaining, underneath are the everlasting arms!

Thus we were able to sing together, at the close of that service, those words of assurance and trust:

> How firm a foundation, ye saints of the Lord,
> Is laid for your faith in His excellent Word!
> What more can He say than to you He hath said,
> To you who for refuge to Jesus have fled?
>
> The soul that on Jesus hath leaned for repose,
> I will not, I will not desert to his foes;
> That soul, tho all hell should endeavor to shake,
> I'll never, no never, no never forsake!

GEORGE KEITH

10

The Lure of a Lesser Loyalty

I WAS HARDLY PREPARED for what I heard that morning. It was the forenoon session of the annual Founder's Week conference at the Moody Bible Institute. Dr. Will Houghton, its honored president, was the Lord's messenger that hour. In the course of his address, he shared an intimate experience he had had some years earlier with his predecessor, Dr. James M. Gray. The two of them had been together in conference, and as they prepared to part, they had joined in a word of prayer. To Dr. Houghton's amazement, he heard his quiet, dignified colleague pray, "O God, don't let me become a wicked old man!"

By his own confession, it took Dr. Houghton by surprise. But if it surprised him, it surprised me even more, for I was quite certain, in those early days of ministry, that as one grew older, he grew more heavenward! But like other lessons that can be learned only through the crucible of personal experience, I discovered that it is not always so, and that we must maintain eternal vigilance in our relationship with God if we are to wear well to the end!

There is an Old Testament story which addresses itself to this particular area of need and does so in a manner which can hardly be ignored. The text is in 1 Kings, chapter 2, beginning at verse 28, and reads as follows:

> Then tidings came to Joab: for Joab had turned after Adonijah, though he turned not after Absalom. And Joab fled unto the tabernacle of the LORD, and caught hold on the horns of

70

the altar. And it was told king Solomon that Joab was fled unto the tabernacle of the LORD; and, behold, he is by the altar. Then Solomon sent Benaiah the son of Jehoiada, saying, Go, fall upon him. . . .So Benaiah the son of Jehoiada went up, and fell upon him, and slew him: and he was buried in his own house in the wilderness.

Having read the text, it would not be surprising if the immediate reaction was not, "So what?" The answer to that question hinges very materially on our knowledge of the chief character, Joab. This man appears first in public life in the narrative of David's wars with Ishbosheth, the son of Israel's first king, Saul. Later, Joab became David's general of the army—the Eisenhower or MacArthur of his day. Dr. Merrill F. Unger says of Joab that he "appears in history as one of the most accomplished and unscrupulous warriors Israel ever produced." Without doubt, he was a national hero.

The biblical citations of his military genius support all that we have said about him, most particularly in reference to his consuming passion for the life and person of David in times of great crisis. It is with these times of special hazard that we are now concerned.

As a start, there was the case of Abner. Second Samuel, chapter 3 reports the incident. Abner had been Saul's commander-in-chief, and together they were the avowed enemies of David, as is well known. But Saul died, and Ishbosheth, his son, succeeded him. Sometime afterward, a misunderstanding developed between the men; Abner became displeased, and he ultimately deserted to David's ranks.

Meanwhile, Joab was away from headquarters on a military expedition and knew nothing of Abner's sudden acceptance into David's favor. Upon his return, however, he received the information, and without delay made himself personally responsible for the removal of Abner. The text cites his obituary: "Joab took him aside in the gate to speak with him quietly, and smote him there under the fifth rib, that he died" (2 Sa 3:27). It is plain that Joab considered Abner such a dangerous threat to the king that he felt no restraint in putting him to death.

The same book of 2 Samuel supplies another sample of the fanatical devotion of Joab to his friend. This time we see him protecting his monarch in his darkest hour. The narrative is preserved for us in 2 Samuel, chapter 11. David had committed adultery with Bathsheba, wife of Uriah. When he learned that his folly might become open scandal, he summoned a messenger with a royal communique for Joab: "Send me Uriah the Hittite" (v. 6). The king's word was his command, and Joab obeyed at once and without a query. What followed is yet another dark chapter in the sad story of David's life at this time. When David learned that he could not manipulate Uriah, for he was an honorable man, David conceived a more sinister scheme; he would have Uriah put to death. And Joab would do it! Whereupon, a second communique was issued in the king's name which read: "Set ye Uriah in the forefront of the hottest battle, and retire ye from him, that he may be smitten, and die" (v. 15).

The record of Scripture assures us that Joab did as he was commanded. He assigned Uriah to a place where he knew valiant men were, and in the battle which ensued, Uriah was slain. The work was done, thanks to Joab. David was safe now, for dead men tell no tales.

The Word of God declares that a "threefold cord is not quickly broken" (Ec 4:12). To complete the preliminary record, we supply a third incident, recorded again in 2 Samuel, chapter 18, and in this case involving David's own flesh and blood. Absalom, David's son, was a choice young man with an obvious charisma that drew people to him. In due course, this charm precipitated a division in the kingdom, and war was the result. As the battle was about to be joined at Mount Ephraim, David drew aside his three generals, Joab among them, and gave this briefing: "Deal gently for my sake with the young man, even with Absalom" (v. 5).

The people were privy to the king's word, and in that knowledge they went out into the field against Israel.

Somehow, in the course of the confusion, Absalom met the servants of David and took flight on his mule. His escape was thwarted, however, when he found his famous locks entangled in the thick boughs of an oak tree and the mule that had been under him gone away. It was at that point that one of the men saw what had happened and reported to Joab. This incensed the general so that he lashed out at the young man, "And why didst thou not smite him to the ground?" (v. 11). With that, Joab hurried off to the place where Absalom hung suspended in the air and thrust three darts through the heart of Absalom while he was still alive in the oak. And there he died.

Our threefold cord bears indisputible witness to the fact that Joab's consuming passion for David knew no bounds; he would do anything to protect the person of the king.

And yet! Look again at the opening words of our text: "Then tidings came to Joab: for Joab had *turned after Adonijah*, though he turned not after Absalom" (1 Ki 2:28). The inspired commentary on this tragic turn of events is preserved for us in 1 Kings 1, beginning at verse 5: "Then Adonijah the son of Haggith exalted himself, saying, I will be king: and he prepared him chariots and horsemen, and fifty men to run before him. . . .And he conferred with Joab the son of Zeruiah, and with Abiathar the priest: and they following Adonijah, helped him." Now read further: "But Zadok the priest, and Benaiah the son of Jehoiada, and Nathan the prophet, and Shimei, and Rei, and the mighty men which belonged to David, were not with Adonijah."

One cannot read that catalog of distinguished men in verse 8 without asking the inevitable question, Why wasn't Joab in that number? That is where he belonged! Having served with such distinction, he deserved to be counted among David's mightiest men. But alas! He had deserted David's ranks in favor of one of David's renegade sons, Adonijah, the son of Haggith.

How could Joab have done this? What had happened? What had consummated the breach? We may ask the questions, but the Scriptures are silent in this case to supply the answers. The incident stands in all its stark reality, the lure of a lesser loyalty. And when the story is told, this great general died in dishonor and was buried, not in Israel's "Arlington National Cemetery," where he should have been interred with full military honors, but in his own house in the wilderness!

It is a sad story, and one which many would like to dismiss as "just one of those things." But in point of fact, what happened to Joab cannot be so easily dismissed, not only because of what happened to a distinguished man in another generation, but because this is not an isolated incident in any generation! The perceptive student of Scripture cannot lightly ignore the repetitious expressions which appear at frequent intervals throughout the sacred text. The psalmist wrote in one place concerning Israel, "Yet they tempted and provoked the most high God, and kept not his testimonies: but *turned back*" (Ps 78:56-57). Or consider this word; "From that time many of his disciples *went back*, and walked no more with him" (Jn 6:66). Or this indictment of the Galatian church, "Ye *did* run well; who did hinder you?" (Gal 5:7). Or the sad word about Demas, "Demas hath *forsaken* me" (2 Ti 4:10). The evidence is there.

The warning should be clear and convincing. The lure of a lesser loyalty knows no limits. It may strike individuals. It may afflict churches. It may endanger institutions. None is exempt from the allurement of some craven Adonijah which can turn us! In *My Utmost for His Highest*, Oswald Chambers serves notice to us all in his word, "Always remain alert to the fact where one man has gone back is exactly where anyone may go back. . . .You have gone through the big crisis, now be alert over the least things; take into calculation the 'retired spheres of the leasts.'" That is a word in season—any season!

Robert Robinson was born in England more than two

hundred years ago. He lost his father at an early age, and his widowed mother sent the boy to London to learn a trade as a barber. There he came under the persuasive influence of George Whitefield, was soundly converted, and began at once to study for the ministry. At twenty-five he was called to the pastorate of the Baptist Church at Cambridge, where he became quite popular. This was the beginning of his lapse into careless ways and his eventual succumbing to his own Adonijah.

It came about on this wise. In the old coaching days, a lady seated on the stagecoach was reading a little book with evident enjoyment. One page of that volume held special appeal to her, and she consulted it from time to time. Turning to her fellow passenger, a gentleman who, she presumed, was acquainted with the subject of religion, she held the open page toward him, and pointing to the hymn she had been reading, asked what he thought of it. The stranger looked at the first few lines:

> Come, Thou Fount of every blessing,
>   Tune my heart to sing Thy grace;
> Streams of mercy, never ceasing,
>   Call for songs of loudest praise.

The stranger read no further, but turned away, endeavoring to engage the lady's attention in something else. But she was not to be denied. Venturing another appeal, she told the man of the benefit she had received from the hymn, and expressed her admiration for its message. With that, overcome beyond the power of controlling his feelings, the stranger burst into tears. "'Madam,' he said, 'I am the poor unhappy man who wrote that hymn many years ago, and I would give a thousand worlds, if I had them, to enjoy the feelings I then had.'"

That stranger was Robert Robinson.

How ironic that, in the end of that hymn, Robinson seemed to prophesy his own zigzag course when he wrote,

> Prone to wander, Lord, I feel it,
> Prone to leave the God I love.

And so he did, and he died in defeat at the age of fifty-five![1] Joab's story has been preserved for our admonition. Scripture and experience confirm the fact that here is a matter which we must not treat with indifference. The stakes are much too high!

Wherein lies our safety? Perhaps the Spirit of God anticipated this very danger when He led the writer to the letter of Hebrews to pen these words: "Wherefore seeing we also are compassed about with so great a cloud of witnesses, let us lay aside every weight, and the sin which doth so easily beset us [could that be the craven Adonijah?], and let us run with patience the race that is set before us, looking unto Jesus" (Heb 12:1:2).

There is the shoe: laying aside the lure and looking unto the Lord!

11

The Hair Can Grow Again

DAVID FALVEY had a painful memory of his aged father's death. The old man, more weakened than anyone realized, had forgotten to perform a very small chore—closing the barnyard gate. When David returned home that evening, weary from the day's work, he found the cattle trampling upon the lawn. He answered his father's greeting with a sharp reprimand, as had become a habit with him. An hour later, sorry for his burst of temper, David determined to make amends and returned to the side porch where the old man had been sitting. But in the interval, the old man had passed away, leaving his sorrows behind.

As time passed, the memory of what he had done haunted David. "One day, he could bear it no longer, and he sobbed, 'Oh, God that was horrible. I was brutish. There was no excuse in the world for it. I didn't have enough quality in me to act as a son should act: I ought to have laughed and said, "Never mind, Dad! It's all right!" But I was just *too little*. And I'm still the same way. O God, help me! In Christ's dear name, heal me!"[1]

To those who have experienced divine forgiveness through Jesus Christ, this story comes home with special meaning. For like David Falvey, we, too, have often failed in word and deed as Christians. It is in such straits that we repair to the throne of grace, wondering if He can ever again restore us to family fellowship and service. There are those who aver it cannot be. It was Aldous L. Huxley who wrote, "The unseen opponent in the great game of life, while scrupulously fair, will allow *no back moves*, and makes us pay in full for every blunder."

While it is true that there is in the Christian life that element which makes back moves difficult, back moves *are possible*. And in the end, there can be restoration to family fellowship and service.

Consider the case of Samson, the son of Manoah, of the family of the Danites.

All the world believes it knows the whole story of Samson. Some there are who treat it as an excellent piece of Hebrew folklore. Beginning with what they imagine was the secret of his greatness, his astonishing strength and feats of prowess, they have produced their own Atlas or Hercules. Not being content to leave it at that, they have embellished the man's history with legends of romance which have reduced him to a man of like passions with themselves. This is the world's view of Samson.

There are others, preachers and commentators in this case, who go to great lengths to compare Samson with the Saviour. "Hanging great weights on small wires," they pick and choose certain incidents in Samson's life, and then declare in so many words, "He is like Him!"

But there is a more excellent way, and certainly more profitable. It is the way in which the apostle Paul handled these Old Testament characters. He expressed his method in these familiar words, "Now all these things happened unto them for examples: and they are written for our admonition, upon whom the ends of the world are come" (1 Co 10:11). You see, in avoiding the mythical and the mystical, the apostle directs us to the practical application which the experiences of these men and women bring to our lives. It is just here that Samson speaks so significantly.

Alexander Whyte seems to say it all when he writes of this man in *Bible Characters*, "What more could God, or man, or angel of God have done for Samson that was not done? . . . From his birth. . .the gifts of God were simply showered on Samson." This is so. Even his name seems to confirm this; it means "sunny." This fact alone may account for the way in which his own people looked upon him—a man with an inexhaustible disposition which buoyed him up in times of great danger and difficulty. Whyte tells us that this disposition was born out of a lightheartedness "with which he fought against countless odds; in his taste for witty sayings and riddles; and in the gigantic practical jokes he perpetuated in carrying off the gates of Gaza, and in tying the foxes tail to tail, and sending them through the standing corn with burning brands."

Samson was clearly a *child of destiny*. This is the foremost thing to be said about him.

But he was more than that. We cannot really explain this paradoxical character without some reference to his *unique distinctive* in preparation for his ministry as Israel's judge. In Judges 13:5, we read, "The child shall be a Nazarite unto God from the womb." To understand the meaning of this statement we must consult the biblical commentary set forth earlier, in the book of Numbers, chapter 6. There the principle is stated and the conditions detailed. The principle of the Nazarite vow was essentially separation unto God. This was basic. And incidentally, it is still basic where the subject of biblical separation is involved. Having settled that matter, we see the conditions laid down: "He shall separate himself from wine and strong drink" (v. 3), that is, be disciplined in his appetites. "There shall no razor come upon his head" (v. 5), that is, he shall be different in his appearance. And finally, "He shall come at no dead body" (v. 6), that is, he shall be distinctive in his associations. Anyone seeing Samson would say, "That man is God's man; he is a Nazarite, set apart unto Jehovah."

It was in this unique relationship to Jehovah that Samson's strength lay! His strength was not brute or natural; it was supernatural, inseparably bound up with his early fidelity to Jehovah. He was to keep himself pure as God's instrument; he was not to yield his members to evil, but to nurture his life in severity and simplicity, and from that discipline, his whole spirit, soul, and body derived its true strength. And for some twenty years, Samson's people saw in this man the unmistakable stamp of the Spirit's enabling.

But as it has happened before, so it happened to Samson; he was slain in his high places! Opportunities do not crown the man. It is what he does with his destiny and with his distinctive that determines how he will do!

This brings us to Judges, chapter 14, and the ominous word, "And Samson went down to Timnath, and saw a woman in Timnath of the daughters of the Philistines. And he came up, and told his father and his mother, and said, I have seen a woman in Timnath of the daughters of the Philistines: now therefore get her for me to wife. . .for she pleaseth me well!" (Judg 14:1-3). In *Bible Characters*, Whyte has wisely observed that Samson's "father and mother never saw another happy day after that day when their son—miraculous birth, Nazarite vow and all—went down to Timnath. . .and said 'Get her for me to wife.'"

There began the tragic *trail of defection*. There we find the key to the progressive deterioration of this great man. Once self-gratification had begun its deadly work, it was but a short journey to Gaza and Delilah. It was there and with her that he gave away the secret of his strength: "There hath not come a razor upon mine head; for I have been a Nazarite unto God from my mother's womb: if I be shaven, then my strength will go from me, and I shall become weak, and be like any other man" (Judg 16:17). Delilah knew that at long last Samson had told her the whole truth. The court barber was summoned; the locks were cut, and Samson was robbed! He may have looked more handsome with his hair cut, but he had lost his power with God and with men. "Flaccid and powerless, he sank a pitiable prey to the ground," observes James Hastings. And so, at long last, Samson tasted the bitter medicine which is spooned off to those who yield to temptation, for at that moment of seizure by the Philistines, he was taken to Gaza, where his eyes were put out, his arms bound with fetters, and he was put to grinding in the prisonhouse.

Surely the Spirit of God would remind us that the way of the transgressor is hard! As R. E. O. White says in *Seed Thoughts for Christian Living*, "This is a world where evil matters, and God deals with it; where as a man sows, so shall he reap; where morality is fundamental, built into the frame of things; and where, though mercy triumphs in the end, it is neither cheap, nor blind, nor stupid."

So Samson discovered. His chastisement was not only severe; it was suited to his sin. Inasmuch as his eyes had been the avenue through which lust had first entered, it was his eyes which were now given to destruction. As Gaza had been the scene of his sin, so Gaza was the scene of his punishment. It all adds up to one solemn lesson for us all: there is nothing vague about divine discipline!

But the story is not finished! Samson's story of destiny, distinction, and defection would not be complete without another word. It is *that* word which, by the input of inspiration, gives rise to hope and the assurance that there may be some back moves with blessing! All this would be impossible were the story to end with Judges 16:21. But there is more, thank God! Judges 16:22 introduces the delightful surprise: "Howbeit the hair of his head began to grow again after he was shaven." It almost sounds as though the Holy Spirit were anticipating that word from the chief of sinners, who declared, "But where sin abounded, grace did much more abound" (Ro 5:20). It was true, something was taking place *naturally* in Samson's body, but something else was happening *spiritually* in his soul. Those blinded eyes, now wet with the tears of sorrow and confession of sin, were lifted heavenward, and Samson was praying now, and like David Falvey was saying, "O Lord GOD, remember me, I pray thee. . .strengthen me."

In his deep humiliation and repentance, the broken vessel was not deserted by his Lord. And for a very basic reason! Judgment is not God's last word to His man! Love is the last, as it is the first. This is not to suggest for one moment that Samson's defection did not create a divine dilemma. On the one hand, there was the thing which God *ought* to do—give him up!

> If I were God
> And man made a mire
> Of things: war, hatred,
> Murder, lust, cobwebs
> Of infamy, entangling
> The heart and soul—
> I would sweep him
> To one side, and start anew
>   (I think I would.)
> If I did this, would I be God? [2]
>
> CARL WEIST

That is what God ought to have done with Samson. But that is not, in fact, what God did do with His friend. While His love will not let us off, neither will it let us go!

This explains David. And Jonah. And Peter.

This gives personality to the potter's vessel in Jeremiah's prophecy, where we read, "And the vessel that he made of clay was marred in the hand of the potter: so *he made it again* another vessel, as seemed good to the potter to make it" (Jer 18:4).

And this gives promise to the plagued land to which the prophet Joel cried, "Fear not, O land; be glad and rejoice: for the LORD will do great things. I will *restore* to you the years that the locust hath eaten" (Joel 2:21, 25).

It is true, then, the hair *can* grow again! Therein lay Samson's hope and the hope of every contrite heart.

This brings us to the *dramatic deliverance*. On a certain day, the Philistines were gathered together in the house of Dagon, their fish god. It was to this god that they offered their sacrifices, and they rejoiced and praised the one who had delivered their enemy into their hands. Not only did they use this occasion to mock Samson; they mocked Samson's God! At last the cry surged through the great hall, "Call for

Samson!" In due course, the victim appeared, feeling his way cautiously, leaning on the arm of a lad who held him by the hand. As soon as the vast throng of lords and ladies saw their erstwhile enemy, the shout of victory was heard: "Long live Dagon, who has delivered Samson into our hands!" And they made sport of him.

Meanwhile, beneath those pillars stood a humbled man of God, quite impervious to all that they were saying about him now. He had higher business. Behold, he prayeth! "O Lord GOD, remember me, I pray thee, and strengthen me, I pray thee, only this once, O God, that I may be at once avenged of the Philistines for my two eyes" (Judg 16:28). With that done, he reached out to the two middle pillars upon which the house stood, to the one with his right hand, to the other with his left. And then, with one last petition, he pushed, and the great house fell upon the lords and upon all the people therein. "So the dead," Scripture affirms, "whom he slew at his death were more than they whom he slew in his life" (v. 30).

In the familiar lines of Hezekiah Butterworth, there are two significant *but*s which bear upon this high and holy moment, not only as they relate to Samson, but to all who skid along the way. Wrote the poet,

> *But* the bird with the broken pinion
> Never soared so high again.

That was the first verse, and if the poet had stopped there, we would be obliged to return to Huxley, and pronounce him right. But that is not the whole truth, for Butterworth went on to write,

> *But* the bird with the broken pinion
> Kept another from the snare,
> And the life that sin had striken
> Raised another from despair.
> Each loss has its compensations,
> There is healing for every pain!

> Though the bird with the broken pinion
> Never soars so high again.

As noble as that second *but* may be in Butterworth's verse, it still falls short of the text which is the truth. Better far to have said at the end of that verse.

> The bird with the broken pinion
> Will soar yet higher still!

It was so with Samson! And it may be so with us, for, "If we confess our sins, he is faithful and just to forgive us our sins, and to cleanse us from all unrighteousness" (1 Jn 1:9).

12

When His Rough Wind Blows

THOMAS CARLYLE used to say that the easy, chatty optimism of Ralph Waldo Emerson maddened him, for no really dark shadow had ever fallen across Emerson's sheltered life. He said that Emerson seemed to him like a man who, standing well back from the least touch of spray, throws chatty observations on the beauty of the weather to a poor man battling for his life in huge waves that are beating him and threatening all the while to sweep him away.

Perhaps Carlyle was right about Emerson; we cannot say. But if personal experience in the marketplace of human relations is of any help, then I am compelled to believe that somewhere along the journey between sunrise and sunset, even Emerson had his share of shadows and felt the rough wind in his face. Misfortune, in one form or another, is the only "international currency" this world has ever known. It is a shoe that all must wear sometime. It is a wise man, therefore, who thatches his house in calm weather so that the storm does not catch him unprepared.

But why the storm at all? It is a reasonable question. "The inquisitive mind," wrote V. Raymond Edman in *Storms and Starlight*, "almost overwhelmed by fierce blast and foaming billows, by darkness of clouds and dimness of courage, [is] quick to ask questions—Why? Whence? By whom? How? To what end?" While it is true that life, to be properly understood, should be reduced to its basic essentials wherever possible, yet there are times in life when oversimplification can be hazardous, even cruel. Especially is this true in the delicate area of life's storms which break upon the body and soul of the Christian. If we are not careful here, we may resort to the smug conclusion of the disciples who, upon observing the man born blind, asked what they thought was the only obvious question in such a case: "Master, who did sin, this man, or his parents, that he was born blind?" (Jn 9:2). It is easy enough to stand in judgment on a blind man when we have good eyesight, or to cast aspersions on the spiritual condition of another who may be ill or afflicted while we enjoy good health. But let it be said, while disobedience and defection may be reasons for divine discipline—and only God can truly judge—they are not the sole reasons for suffering and affliction in the believer's life.

I am constrained to write out of a measure of personal involvement in this arena, not as an expert, but from some experience. Like many of my colleagues in the pastoral ministry, I accepted the visitation of the sick, the afflicted, and the dying as a legitimate part of my shepherd task. In those more than three decades, I have sat where they have sat and have seen the invasion of disease and death as they relentlessly robbed my sheep.

But now I am experiencing something of that invasion in my own body. I write these lines only because of the faithfulness of my heavenly Father and the mechanical means of an artificial kidney machine. I am literally plugged in for life! Through all these experiences I have come to believe that to ask why to human suffering is neither surprising nor sinful. I have found comfort in the fact that even Paul had his fainting fit and was not ashamed to speak of it in writing to the Corinthians. "We are handicapped on all sides," he wrote, "but we are never frustrated; we are puzzled, but never in despair. We are persecuted, but we never have to stand it alone: we may be knocked down but we are never knocked out! Every day we experience something of the death of Jesus, so that we may also know the power of the life of Jesus in these bodies of ours (2 Co 4:8-10, Phillips).

And so it has come to pass that His rough wind has blown my way.

It blew initially in a Chicago hospital during midwinter. Beside me lay Vance Havner's little volume, *It is Toward Evening*, a gift from a friend. I am convinced it was another hand on mine which led me to the chapter on the boll weevil, in which Havner relates the story of a certain southern town which made its living by raising cotton. But the boll weevil invaded that little community, devastating the cotton crop, and threatening to put everyone in the poorhouse. The farmers were an ingenious lot, however. They planted peanuts and other produce which eventually brought them more money than they had ever made raising cotton. In the end, what had seemed a disaster, at first, turned into a boon, and to show their appreciation of the incident which had seemed like an accident they erected a monument to the boll weevil. I suppose it still stands in that town to this day.

That much of the story was history; now came the application, as only Vance Havner can make it. My friend began,

> "All things work together for good" to the Christian, even our boll weevil experiences. Sometimes we settle into a humdrum routine as monotonous as growing cotton year after year. Then God sends the boll weevil; He jolts us out of our groove, and we must find new ways to live. Financial reverses, great bereavement, physical infirmity, loss of position—how many have been driven by trouble to be better husbandmen and to bring forth far finer fruit from their souls! The best thing that ever happened to some of us was the coming of our "boll weevil." Without that we might still have been a "cotton sharecropper."
>
> If the boll weevil has struck your cotton crop, do not despair. The day may come when you will put up a monument to the bane that became a blessing.[1]

In reflection, I believe it was on that dark, cold night that I gathered the brick and mortar for my monument and determined before the Lord to find the blessing from the boll weevil that had invaded my cotton crop. And interestingly enough, in doing so, I made some biblical discoveries which have provided me and some others with a firm foundation for other monuments!

At the outset, let us consider the *organic* aspect of suffering. We could assume here what we ought to assert. Our organic unity with humanity, not only immediately but as far back as Adam, is the culprit here. While it is true that the child of God has new life and a new nature in Christ, he still retains his unbroken physical link with Adam's race, and that means sharing in the fruit of Adam's sin, which was death. "In Adam all die," the Scriptures declare (1 Co 15:22). We may dispute that decree, but it remains one of the most patent facts of life. It was to that indisputable fact that Paul addressed the believers in Rome when he wrote, "Wherefore, as by one man sin entered into the world, and death by sin; and so death passed upon all men, for that all have sinned" (Ro 5:12).

We may ask the question, What is to be my attitude toward this organic union? If we are wise men, we will submit to it, for it cannot be otherwise; it is part of the penalty of being born into this world and being members of the body politic.

There is a second reason for suffering among the saints of God. We may speak of it as *vicarious*, that is, an affliction experienced so that it may be the instrument of comfort to another in similar straits. William Elliott, Jr., raises the question at this point:

> Is it not true that the people to whom you and I instinctively turn in times of deep trouble are those who have suffered, and won a spiritual victory over it? It takes suffering to understand suffering; it takes heartache to appreciate heartache; it takes loneliness to sympathize with loneliness. . . .As the author of Hebrews reminds us: "We have not an high priest which cannot be touched with the feeling of our infirmities; but was in all points tempted like as we are."[2]

It is for precisely the same reason that our heavenly Father permits us to taste suffering and affliction in this life, "that we may be able to comfort them which are in any trouble, by the comfort wherewith we ourselves are comforted of God" (2 Co 1:4). W. E. Sangster is right when he says, "Suffering, in a disciple, can often be wrested to service." How often I have observed God's suffering saints ministering comfort to other sufferers, not because they counted themselves masters in the art of coping with affliction, but simply because they had learned, in the crucible, the comfort of God to their own hearts and were willing to serve others in some need. In some measure, I have experienced this in my own life, while the "thorn" lingers. Now I am able to visit the bedside of the ill and afflicted and say, without the words seeming to mock me, "My friend in Christ, I know something of what you are enduring; I am there!"

So it is, just as Jowett so aptly puts it; "God comforts, not to make us comfortable, but to make us comforters." Let us, then, determine before the Lord that we will be good stewards of this peculiar ministry and will avail ourselves of those opportunities to speak a word in season to those who are passing through the "glen of gloom."

We come, now, to a third aspect of suffering, which is little known or, if it is, little understood. It is that form of suffering which *identifies* us with our Lord Jesus Christ in finalizing His redemptive purpose in the church. We speak carefully here. In the first chapter of Colossians, the apostle interprets the person and work of Jesus Christ and applies these things to the church in Colossae. He does so in the full knowledge of his own personal share in the propogation of the gospel. "Whereof I Paul am made a minister" (Col 1:23) is his manner of describing his ministry. This leads him to set forth a principle of that ministry in which he and all believers share alike; it is the ministry of suffering. From his prison house in Rome, with the chain on his wrist, this bird sings from his darkened cage, "Who now rejoice in my sufferings for you, and fill up that which is behind of the afflictions of Christ in my flesh for his body's sake, which is the church" (Col 1:24).

The question now is critical. Whatever did Paul mean by these words? "Does Paul mean to say," queries Alexander MacLaren, "that in any sense whatever the sufferings which Christ endured had anything 'lacking' in them? or does he mean to say that a Christian man's sufferings, however they may benefit the Church, can be put along-side of the Lord's, and taken to eke out the incompleteness of His?" The answer should be obvious to any instructed believer; there is nothing in our suffering that has anything *atoning* in it! The work of eternal redemption was His alone, and when He cried from the cross, "It is finished," it was finished! That sacrifice needs no supplement, indeed, will receive none.

The issue, then, may be resolved on the basis not of atonement, but of *association*. First, there is the suffering which our Lord feels in the life and suffering of one of His own. As far back as the prophets, we have the principle stated, "In all their affliction he was afflicted" (Is 63:9). Strike the man that is joined to Christ here, and Christ up yonder feels it! Paul learned that lesson as he made his way into Damascus and was arrested with that word from heaven, "Saul, Saul, why persecutest thou me?" Not "them," though that was who Paul had in mind, but "me."

But secondly, and more relevant to this matter, there is the association which we may have with our Lord in bringing to full term those who are to be added to the family of God by means of the new birth, or again, those who can be brought to spiritual maturity by means of our suffering. I think Frank W. Boreham has seized the heart of the problem when he writes,

> If Jesus, the Son of God, had died His bitter death on Calvary's tree, and left it at that, would that have saved the world? Of course not. The world at large would never have heard of it. The tragic incident would have passed into oblivion within a year or two. Just another political execution in a Roman province! In order that the redeeming sacrifice might be made effective, and the world saved by means of it, it was necessary for the Apostles to suffer and die in proclaiming it,

for the martyrs to lay down their lives in defending it, and for missionaries like Xavier and Livingstone and Patterson and Williams and Chalmers to seal with their blood their testimony to its virtue. Every such death on a foreign shore, every tear shed for the gospel's sake, every jibe or sneer patiently endured out of love for Christ, is an augmentation of the awful tragedy of Golgotha. It is the wonder of wonders that He who died upon the bitter tree to redeem mankind associates each of us with Himself in that divine and sacrificial work.[3]

It should be no small matter, then, to understand that if we suffer according to the will of God, we do not suffer in vain; it is for His body, which is the Church of God. That makes it all worthwhile and purposeful.

These lead us to consider a fourth form of suffering. I have chosen to call it the work of *maturation*. It addresses itself to this thought: God is not only concerned about the effect of our affliction and suffering in *others*; He is equally concerned about the effect of those things in *us*. And what is that? In His divine purpose, it is the making of sons like His Son! When we put our hearts to rest on Romans 8:28, we should also put our heads to think on the next verse, "For whom he did foreknow, he did also predestinate to be conformed to the image of his Son."

This is God's purpose, and He will stop at nothing in order to bring it to pass. How beautifully the Scripture speaks of the Redeemer who "shall sit as a refiner and purifier of silver" (Mal 3:3). "Being determined," writes Arthur T. Pierson on this point, "to perfect His saints, He puts His precious metal into His crucible. But He sits by it, and watches it. Love is His thermometer, and marks the exact degree of heat; not one instant's unnecessary pang will He permit; and as soon as the dross is released so that He sees Himself reflected in the fire, the trial ceases."[4]

And finally, we speak of that aspect of suffering without which no treatment of the subject could be complete, it seems. Indeed, it may be that in the sight of God this is the most viable of all: suffering for the *glory of God*.

This thought may help us understand our Lord's bearing toward those two sisters at Bethany, who kept house for their brother, Lazarus. Dear as he was to them, they could not prevent the inevitable illness and eventual death of their brother. Upon learning that Jesus was in the vicinity, the sisters ran to the Saviour with the entreaty, "Lord, behold, he whom thou lovest is sick" (Jn 11:3). When Jesus heard that, He replied, "This sickness is not unto death, but for the glory of God, that the Son of God might be glorified thereby" (v. 4).

We see, at once, that to His discerning, designing providence, there was something more involved in this illness than the mere matter of relieving a sick friend, which is what Lazarus wanted, and for which his sisters pleaded. The glory of God had to be considered. As one of God's servants has written,

> He saw in this case an occasion for the display of the divine glory, and not merely for the exhibition of personal affection, however deep and real that might be—and with Him, surely it was both deep and real, for we read, "Jesus loved Martha and her sister and Lazarus." But in the judgment of our blessed and adorable Lord, the glory of God took precedence of every other consideration. . . .He was ruled in all things by the glory of God. . . .Hence, though it might be a good thing to relieve a friend in distress, it was far better and higher to glorify God; and we may be sure, that the beloved family of Bethany sustained no loss by a delay which only made room for the brighter outshining of the divine glory.[5]

However deep the mystery may appear—and at times it does seem dark, tangled, and inexplicable—yet it is faith's privilege to say through it all, "This sickness, this affliction, this suffering is for the glory of my God."

In his *Daily Readings*, W. E. Sangster has a choice cameo

covering this subject, which should cheer the heart. In
speaking of "Pearls and Pain," the author writes,

> Scientists are agreed that pearls are the product of pain.
> Sometimes the pain is caused by a microscopic worm and
> sometimes by a boring parasite. In this latter case, the shell of
> the oyster or mussel gets pierced, chipped or perforated and
> some alien substance (a speck of sand it may be) gets inside.
> Immediately, all the resources of the tiny organism rush to
> the spot where the breach has been made. On the entry of
> that foreign irritant the unsuspected healing powers of the
> little creature are marshalled at the point of peril. . .powers
> that otherwise would have remained ever dormant are called
> out by this new emergency; the foreign irritant is covered and
> the wound healed—by a pearl. No other gem has so fascinat-
> ing a history. . . .It is the symbol of stress; it is a healed
> wound; it is the enduring token of a tiny creature's struggle to
> preserve its life. We do not normally associate pearls with
> pain. Pearls are for the ballroom; pearls are for the hours of
> entertainment and of relaxation; pearls will share in the
> sparkle and gaiety of those who agree to forget for a while
> that life has its sombre and saddening sides. But pearls are
> not so made! Their history contrasts strangely with their use.
> They are the product not of pleasure, but of pain. They are
> healed wounds. If there had been no wound there could have
> been no pearl. Some oysters are never wounded and the men
> who seek for gems throw them aside.[6]

No surpirse, then, that Peter Marshall observes in *Mr.
Jones, Meet the Master*, "One enters into the presence of
the Lord through gates bedecked with pearls, and every
pearl—a trouble, a pain, a heartache, a misfortune, which,
by the grace of God, has been changed into a beautiful,
lovely thing. No wonder they speak of pearly gates!"

In the meantime, while we wait, let us rest in the promises
and purposes of a faithful God, and as His rough wind blows
at times, pray on,

> Lord, keep me still,
> Though stormy winds may blow.

And waves my little bark may overflow,
Or even if in darkness I must go,
Yet keep me still.

Lord, keep me still;
The waves are in Thy hand,
The roughest winds subside at Thy command,
Stir Thou my bark in safety to the land,
And keep me still, and keep me still.

Author Unknown

13
The River of God

THERE IS AN OLD Spanish proverb which Isaac Walton quotes with a fine smack of approval. "Rivers," he says, "were for wise men to contemplate, and for fools to pass by without contemplation."

Now, the Jews were wise men indeed, but they had no river flowing through their fair capital city of Jerusalem. It was for the want of a river that they never forgave a frowning Providence. "They heard," wrote Boreham, "how Babylon stood proudly surveying the shining waters of the Euphrates, how Ninevah was beautified by the lordly Tigris, how Thebes glittered in stately grandeur on the Nile, and how Rome sat in state beside the Tiber; and they were consumed with envy because no broad river protected them from their foes, and bore to their gates the wealthy merchandise of many lands."[1]

This may explain why it was that the riverless prophets and psalmists wrote so longingly and lavishly about them. Where can we find a more glowing example than that word from the prophet Isaiah, "But there the glorious LORD will be unto us a place of broad rivers and streams; wherein shall go no galley with oars, neither shall gallant ship pass thereby" (Is 33:21).

We are not proposing a nature study, however. Rivers are mentioned only because of what they suggest in the larger and later symbolism of our Lord's own teaching on the subject.

It is essential that we begin our journey with a visit to the headwaters of the river as set forth in Ezekiel's vision, chapter 47. After a look around and a careful perusal of the riverbed, we must rest awhile in order to consider the deeper meaning of it all in the light of some words spoken by the Saviour many years later, during the course of one of His sermons. It was the last day of the feast of tabernacles. Jesus stood and cried, "If any man thirst, let him come unto me, and drink. He that believeth on me, as the scripture hath said, out of his belly shall flow rivers of living water. (But this spake he of the Spirit, which they that believe on him should receive: for the Holy Ghost was not yet given; because that Jesus was not yet glorified)" (Jn 7:37-39).

As we pause here, observe two things. First, our Lord clearly identifies water with the Holy Spirit; the one is a symbol of the other, which is the reality. And second, this member of the Godhead, the Holy Spirit, is received by all who receive the Saviour. We must be clear on these matters if we are to benefit from what follows.

Now, taking Ezekiel's river together with the Saviour's symbolism, we go a step further and add a perceptive phrase from Paul's epistle to the Philippians, where he speaks of "the supply of the Spirit" (Phil 1:19).

Here, then, is the stream; its symbolism; and its supplies. From these channels of truth, three principal tributaries emerge and flow downstream.

Mark first the *means* of the supply. In the opening words of the prophet's vision, he cites this important fact, "The waters came down from under the right side of the house, at the south side of the altar" (v. 1). The word "altar" is critical to all that follows, for it reminds us at once that this stream draws its source from sacrifice. It was there on the north side that all the sacrifices were slain. The vision verifies the fact that in the larger meaning of the terminology employed by the prophet, Calvary precedes Pentecost! It must be ever thus! Stephen Olford confirms this, when he says, "If you would know the experience of Pentecost in your life, know that the outflow of the Holy Spirit only flows where there is an altar. You must first know this Christ of Calvary, and accept His dying there for you. Then you must go on to know the cross in your life, accepting the sentence of the cross upon all that is of self. . . . The altar is the place of death to sin and self."

What a needful word! And how little it is understood by the rank and file of God's people. Only occasionally does one find a child of God who sees the initial meaning of the cross and its integrating message as a part of the whole saving experience. But it is all there at the altar.

In my privileged days of association with Scofield Memorial Church, I saw an army of God's giants come and go in ministry there. One such was William R. Newell, whose volumes on Romans, Hebrews, and the Revelation have helped so many to understand these critical books. That dear servant of God was sharing his early life with us in one of his evening studies. He confessed his anxiety after holiness, and how, in desperation for all that he felt God had for him, he had made a visit to D. C. Hoste, successor to Hudson Taylor, founder of the China Inland Mission, to pour out his desire to him. "O, Mr. Hoste," he said, "pray that I may be nothing!" To which Mr. Hoste replied in his typical, high-pitched voice, "Will, you *are* nothing; take it by faith!"

That is the message of the means of the supply of the Spirit.

This brings us to consider the *measure* of that supply. The word translated *supply* in the Philippian passage suggests *plenty*. More than one translator takes the word to mean "a rich provision." As applied in this situation, the reservoir is inexhaustible! Look at the interesting figures employed by the prophet beginning at verse 3. "And when the man that had the line in his hand went forth eastward, he measured a thousand cubits, and he brought me through the waters; the waters were to the *ankles*." Recall the lame beggar who felt the healing touch of Peter and John in Acts 3? Something very pertinent took place at the moment of his healing. The text tells us that Peter took the beggar by the right hand and lifted him up; "And immediately his feet and ankle bones received strength. And he leaping up stood, and walked (Ac 3:7-8).

Does this not provide us with a fitting figure of walking in the Spirit? That initial experience that comes to the child of God once he receives new life in Jesus Christ—he walks! This suggests motion, direction in life. And how does one do this? "This I say then, Walk in the Spirit" (Gal 5:16).

But there is more. "Again he measured a thousand, and brought me through the waters; the waters were to the *knees*" (v. 4). There is a suggestive word from Paul's Ephesian epistle. After leading his readers to the summit and enabling them to see the eternal purpose of God, which He purposed in Jesus Christ and revealed to the church, Paul goes on to write, "For this cause I bow my knees unto the Father of our Lord Jesus Christ" (Eph 3:14).

Could this be praying in the Spirit? One does not look far into the writings of the apostles before he finds these very words used: "Praying always with all prayer and supplication in the Spirit" (Eph 6:18) and "praying in the Holy Ghost" (Jude 20).

Once again the measuring line is employed, and this time, "the waters were to the *loins*" (v. 4). There is an appropriate word in Genesis just here. Jehovah is addressing His servant Jacob, and speaks as follows: "I am God Almighty: be fruitful and multiply; a nation and a company of nations shall be of thee, and kings shall come out of thy loins" (Gen 35:11). It seems that what God promised Jacob physically, He purposes spiritually for us—fruitfulness in the Spirit. "But the fruit of the Spirit," wrote Paul to the Galatians, "is love, joy, peace, longsuffering, gentleness, goodness, faith, meekness, temperance" (Gal 5:22-23).

But the end is not yet! Once again, "he measured a thousand; and it was a river that I could not pass over: for the waters were risen, waters to *swim in*, a river that could not be passed over." Here surely we have the fullness of the Spirit, or more accurately, the realization of what Paul meant when he commanded the Ephesians to "be filled with the Spirit" (Eph 5:18).

Skevington Wood seems to have put it all together for us when he wrote,

> Can we capture a vision from the Scriptures of God's over-flowing reservoir of spiritual replenishment available to us in the Holy Ghost? And can we contrast the inexhaustibility of this ever-fresh supply with the poverty of our own disciple-ship? The question with which God confronts us here is this: Am I living up to the limit of what God makes possible for me in the Holy Spirit?. . .So far from claiming God's utmost we are pathetically content to paddle in the pools left behind by the tide, when we might be enjoying waters to swim in.[3]

This brought to mind some words which I heard first many years ago during a breakfast-table devotional at Gull Lake Bible Conference. The layman who shared them with us seemed to me to be calling us to an experience which he himself had come to enjoy, and therefore the impact was impressive. Here was what he recited that morning:

> Art thou *paddling*, fellow Christian,
> In God's sea of boundless grace?
> Are thy ankles merely covered
> When He bids to shoreless space?
> Is your diet still a milk one,
> When He offers you the meat?
> Venture forth, my timid brother,
> Let Him bathe beyond thy feet.

> Art thou *wading*, fellow Christian,
> In His grace, so full and free?
> Have you had the joy of knowing
> That the tide has reached thy knee?
> Have you found that prayer's a weapon?
> We may wield it, if we will.
> To your growing heart He whispers
> "Venture on; go farther still."

Art thou *bathing*, fellow Christian,
In the ocean of His love?
Have thy loins been wholly covered
By His grace, who reigns above?
Do you find the peace and power,
When the tempter comes your way?
Do you see God's hand still leading
As He guides you day by day?

Art thou *swimming*, fellow Christian,
With no foothold on the sand?
With no trust in self relying,
Held by His almighty hand?
Do you rest in Him completely
When the trials vex you sore?
They are meant to draw you to Him!
Come, oh come, and trust Him more!
                    GRACE L. HAGEMANN

This brings us to the last bend in the river, where we pause to consider the *ministry* of the supply. The results of the river's flow were thrilling! Wherever the river went, things happened. We read in verse 9, "Every thing. . .whithersoever the rivers shall come, shall live: and there shall be a very great multitude of fish, because these waters shall come thither: for they shall be healed; and every thing shall live whither the river cometh. . . .and the fruit thereof shall be for meat, and the leaf thereof for medicine" (Eze 47:9, 12).

What a ministry! Life! Healing! Medicine! Surely these are the things which God intended should issue out from these lives of ours. Ours is meant to be a ministry of *life*. God is not so interested in a point of view as He is in a relationship of life. It is that new life in Jesus Christ that God the Holy Spirit wants to bring to those who sit in darkness and the shadow of death. And He wants to bring healing to the many brokenhearted who sit on society's roadside. Unfortunately, in all too many instances, we have nothing to give them. We must acknowledge the prophet's indictment,

"Thou hast no healing medicines" (Jer 30:13). But we ought to have! And we may have, if we will allow the Spirit of God to do His peculiar work in our lives.

The vision includes an appeal which we must not ignore. In verse 6, the heavenly messenger says to the prophet, "Son of man, hast thou seen this?"

Are we willing to ask ourselves that question? Have I experienced this? Am I clear on the *means* of the supply of the Spirit—no Spirit without the sacrifice of Calvary? Am I now experiencing daily something of the waters—to the ankles, to the knees, to the loins, and waters to swim in? And what of my *ministry*, or better, His ministry through me? Are living relationships being established; are hearts finding healing through a touch with my life?

A. W. Tozer touched the vital nerve when he wrote in *The Divine Conquest*, "When the Holy Spirit ceases to be incidental and again becomes fundamental the power of the Spirit will be asserted once more among the people called Christians."

14
We're Marching to Zion

THE YOUTHFUL ZECHARIAH was a prophet of Israel. But he was more. He was a zealous patriot. Born during the Babylonian captivity, the son of a prominent priest, Zechariah learned early something of the harsh realities of life. He also cherished those aspirations for the future which were the birthright of every true son of Israel. To his prophetic task, therefore, he brought both the insight of a man able to speak to his times and the inspiration of a man able to see beyond his times to that final travail and triumph of Zion, when even the bells on the horses and the pots in the kitchens shall be "HOLINESS UNTO THE LORD" (Zec 14:20).

It is from this man's prophetic oracle, then, that we take our marching orders.

"Turn you to the strong hold, ye prisoners of hope:" he begins, "even to day do I declare that I will render double unto thee: when I have bent Judah for me, filled the bow with Ephraim, and raised up thy sons, O Zion, against thy sons, O Greece, and made thee as the sword of a mighty man" (Zec 9:12-13).

In a striking figure, the King of Zion is described as an archer who bends a mighty bow. But the arrows which He fits to the string are not the deadly missiles of mechanized warfare usually associated with military operations, but the great forces of conflicting ideologies which manifest themselves in contending personalities, distinguished in our text as the sons of Zion and the sons of Greece.

Our curiosity is immediately aroused. Who are these people? And what do they say to us in our times? It seems reasonable to believe that we should not limit the conflict here to the prophet's own day. That did occur. But the times require that we paint on a larger canvas and see that the warfare between these sons is, in reality, the warfare between the seeds, which was announced at the dawn of man's creation and will continue with us until the kingdoms of this world become the kingdoms of our God and of His Christ!

We speak first of the *sons of Greece*. But why should we concern ourselves with what happened twenty-five centuries ago on a rocky, half-barren, Mediterranean peninsula no larger than the island of Cuba? Simply because the genius of the Greeks laid down for the whole Western world the foundations for the study of government, literature, art, and philosophy. In a word, this people represented the best that humanity could produce to date! And yet, for all the glory that was Greece, there was a grave defect in their corporate character, which made them the most paradoxical people since the dawn of time. As *Life* magazine observed in one of its issues,

> They conceived the first real democracy, yet they kept slaves in it. . .they preached moderation, yet their "fondness for frenzy" shocked the barbarians. . .they were the world's greatest warriors, yet their battle plans were often based on eclipses and the entrails of birds. . .they changed the whole course of civilization, yet they could not change themselves in order to survive. . .they blazed across our planet like a comet, and burned out like one.[1]

How could this be?

Speaking broadly, throughout all the areas of accomplishment in which the sons of Greece excelled, there was a basic, underlying determination to live by the light of reason. The Greeks had a phrase for it, "Nothing to excess." In their sculpture and architecture, in their literature and philosophy, the Greeks were, above all else, reasonable. But it was this suffocating stress on rationalism which blinded them in regard to the future. They were the original "now" generation. "This is paradise enough, heaven can wait," they reasoned. Consequently, tomorrow and its responsibilities did not greatly interest them; they were engrossed in the business of making the most of the present. They were, to borrow an expression from one of David's psalms, "men of the world, which have their portion in this life" (Ps 17:14).

Such were those first sons of Greece.

But the question for us, now, is this; Does all this suggest a modern parallel? Is there any similarity between that ancient civilization and our own? I believe there is. Intimate contacts in the marketplace of our society confirm the fact that the sons of Greece are ever with us! They are the major contemporary force with which we must reckon on every level of our computerized, zip-coded, assembly-line way of life. You meet them in the supermarket. You sit beside them on the jet flight from one place to another. Make no mistake about it, these people, by and large, are cultured, intellectually alert, sophisticated, materially affluent, and often outwardly religious. But they are often non-Christian, sometimes even anti-Christian. Their ground-level philosophy asserts itself in much of our scholarship, which refuses to lay its treasures at the feet of the One in whom are hid all the treasures of wisdom and knowledge; in much of our major news media—magazines, television, and the press, which pander to the base nature of the unregenerate heart; in the immoral and salacious world of entertainment; in the traffic in harmful drugs and alcohol; in organized gambling and corruption, even in high places in government; and in nearly every area of public life where unscrupulous people exploit human weakness for private gain. Whether they are conscious of it or not, the net result has been, and is, the progressive paganization of our society!

T. S. Eliot has described them best:

> Here were decent godless people;
> Their only monument the asphalt road
> And a thousand lost golf balls.[2]

So much for the sons of Greece.

We turn, now, to consider those other combatants in the struggle, identified in the words of the prophet as the "*sons of Zion.*"

Historically, Zion is associated with the ancient capital city of Jerusalem. But the term has a deeper meaning. John Newton saw it in his hymn, "Glorious Things of Thee are Spoken," where he speaks of Zion as the "city of our God." This thought adds a dimension to these sons of Zion which makes them different. In contrast to the sons of Greece, who are children of this world, these sons are the children of God!

Here is a matter with far-reaching implications. For one thing, these sons have a different life. They are men who have received divine life from God through personal faith in His Son, Jesus Christ. Arising from that spiritual starting-point, these sons have a different manner of life. Their Christian commitment results in Christian character with a posture for righteousness, godliness, truth and love. Zechariah describes them appropriately in those words, "The LORD shall be seen over them" (Zec 9:14). And finally, these sons of Zion have a different mission in life. Their enlistment and equipment emerge in engagement! They are going forth into the world to close with the opposition in a struggle for the kingdom of God and the glory of Christ.

I see a long procession of them as they flock to their King, "fair as the moon, clear as the sun, and terrible as an army with banners" (Song 6:10). Foremost among them were those twelve raw recruits, disciples in clay, who were sent out by the young King to preach the gospel to all the world. Not long afterward, other brave sons took up the mantle of ministry, and with bold strokes dared to enter the conflict against the sons of Greece. Their record is dramatically preserved for posterity in the Acts of the Apostles. Can we ever forget that chief son of Zion, the apostle Paul, as he marched through the land? Places like Jerusalem, Antioch, Philippi, Thessalonica, Athens, Corinth, and Rome felt the mighty impact of his witness for Jesus Christ!

But I see others in that procession, in the minority to be sure, but capable of changing the course of history. Speaking of those ancient days of Rome, with its colosseum where sons of Zion died for their faith, Vance Havner pays this fitting tribute:

> If we had sat in those grandstands amidst the "grandeur that was Rome" we might have been deceived. For it was not the howling mob in the Colosseum that determined the course of history. Underground in the catacombs another force was working. A handful of men and women who worshiped another King called Jesus, who had died and risen and was coming back some day—here was the beginning of an empire within an empire, the Christians beneath the Caesars. They crept along the subterranean passageways and tunnels, among the tombs and caverns, hunted and persecuted, the "scum of the earth." If we had prowled around those gloomy depths we might have come on little companies singing, listening to a Gospel message, observing the Lord's Supper. We might have said, "They haven't a chance." But the Christians underground eventually upset the Caesars above ground. The catacombs overcame the Colosseum and finally put the ampitheatre out of business. . . . We cannot forget this fellowship of simple believers who loved Jesus Christ more than their lives, in the world, but not of it, whose blood was the seed of the church. . . . These denizens of God's Underground were on fire with a passion which swords could not kill nor water drown nor fire destroy. Their blood was spilled so freely in the arena that a traveler was asked, "Do you want a relic? Take a handful of sand from the Colosseum. It is all martyrs."[3]

And what shall we say more? For the time would fail to tell of the multitudes who have left our evangelical institutions under sealed orders and today, for the most part, are witnessing a good confession in the world.

But it is just here that I can anticipate the question that someone is certain to raise, But what are these among so many? The sons of Greece are a great multitude; we are a contemptible, little army by comparison. The struggle seems hopelessly unequal.

This may help us. The author of the following lines is unknown, but his experience of standing on an ocean beach and observing the incoming tide, as wave after wave broke on the shore, both answers the questions and provides a fitting illustration.

> On the far reef the breakers recoil in shattered foam;
> Yet still the sea behind them urges its forces home;
> Its chant of triumph surges through all the thunderous din.
> The wave may break in failure, but the tide is sure to win.
>
> O mighty sea, thy message in chanting spray is cast
> Within God's plan of progress, it matters not at last,
> How wide the shores of evil, how strong the reefs of sin;
> The wave may be defeated, but the tide is sure to win.
>
> AUTHOR UNKNOWN

So will it be! The tide of God's divine and progressive purposes for His church and this world are as certain as that Jesus Christ is alive today at the right hand of God! This not to say that in the end all will be the sons of Zion! The scope of Scripture does not teach this, or even imply it. But we are assured that history will have a worthy conclusion in which the sons of Zion will triumph at last over the sons of Greece. Zechariah saw all this, for as he surveyed the future with the clear vision of a true prophet, he concluded his apocalyptic message with this burst of optimism, "And the LORD their God shall save them in that day as the flock of his people" (Zec 9:16). That sounds like victory!

But it is to a warfare that we are called; we must not forget that. It has been billed as "The sons of Zion versus the sons of Greece." As we contribute our share to the crusade, let us read carefully our combat assignments as laid out for us in the Word of God. When the King of Zion was here on earth, He said, "Man shall not live by bread alone, but by every

word that proceedeth out of the mouth of God" (Mt. 4:4).
That counsel will always be relevant.

Again, maintain a philosophy of life which is primarily
vertical in its emphasis. "Seek ye first the kingdom of God,
and his righteousness" was part of the original mandate giv-
en to the children of God (Mt 6:33); it has never been abro-
gated. You will find that by accepting its terms for life, you
hold in your hand the key which will unlock the door behind
which all the other valued keys are kept.

And finally, always appraise this present world, no matter
how attractive it may be, with the insight of divine redemption. This will keep you from being shaken by the breakdown
of humanistic science, materialistic technology, and mere
human wisdom seeking goals by human means. Knowing
that the world is guilty, lost, and helpless, you will, with
open eyes and realistic mind, look to divine initiative for
deliverance.

So, for one brief moment before we set out, let us borrow a
manuscript from that grand old man of sacred music, Isaac
Watts, and let us sing together that "national anthem" which
belongs in a very special way to all true sons of Zion.

> Come, we that love the Lord,
> And let our joys be known,
> Join in a song with sweet accord,
> Join in a song with sweet accord,
> And thus surround the throne,
> And thus surround the throne.
>
> Let those refuse to sing
> Who never knew our God;
> But children of the heavenly King,
> May speak their joys aborad,
> May speak their joys abroad.
>
> The hill of Zion yields
> A thousand sacred sweets
> Before we reach the heav'nly fields,
> Before we reach the heav'nly fields

Or walk the golden streets,
Or walk the golden streets.

Then let our songs abound
And ev'ry tear be dry;
We're marching thru Immanuel's ground,
We're marching thru Immanuel's ground
To fairer worlds on high,
To fairer worlds on high.

We're marching to Zion,
Beautiful, beautiful Zion;
We're marching upward to Zion,
The beautiful city of God.

Wherefore, ye sons of Zion, "be ye steadfast, unmoveable, always abounding in the work of the Lord, forasmuch as ye know that your labour is not in vain in the Lord." (1 Co. 15:58).

15
What Manner of Men?

FAR INTO THE NIGHT, a group of men was sitting together in the lobby of a midwestern hotel. No words were spoken to break the silence. Off in the corner of the lobby, the old grandfather clock suddenly summoned all its strength and, to the astonishment of the silent spectators, struck *thirteen*! Whereupon, one of the old gentlemen rose to his feet and headed for the door. Before leaving the lobby to return to his room, he turned back to his friends and remarked, "Well, I guess I'll be going now; it's later than it's ever been before!"

We may find the old story a bit amusing, but the truth is that the remark of our friend is confirmed by the hard facts of science. The French scientist Pierre Berchelt stated in 1860, in his book, *Re-Entry*, "Inside of one hundred years of physical and chemical science, man will know what the atom is. It is my belief, that when science reaches that stage, God will come down to earth with His big ring of keys, and say to humanity, 'Gentlemen, it's closing time.'"

These are but two samples which seem to suggest that the sands of time are fast running their course and that this age of the astronauts may well be the last before the close of the age of grace and the ultimate dawn of the age of glory!

For the rank and file of humanity, there is neither explanation of what is happening in our world nor expectation of what is yet to come. That distinguished scholar, H.A.L. Fisher, in his book *History of Europe*, reveals the prevailing philosophy when he writes, "Wiser men than I have discerned in history a plot, a rhythm, a predetermined pattern. These harmonies are concealed from me. I can see only one emergency following upon another as wave follows wave."

And T. S. Eliot, in one of his earlier writings, reflected this same pessimism when he wrote,

> This is the way the world ends,
> This is the way the world ends,
> This is the way the world ends,
> Not with a bang but a whimper.[1]

Let this blessed assurance control, the world is not going to end with a whimper. Nor is it going to end with a bang. It is going to end "with a shout, with the voice of the archangel, and with the trump of God" (1 Th 4:16).

In the bright light of this biblical truth, there is a constant need to keep our prophetic shoes in good repair! It often happens that the saints of God spend most of their time on the intricacies of prophecy to the neglect of the *implications* of prophecy. Thus, it is not uncommon to find people avidly gathering for prophetic conferences to bring their charts up to date, while in reality, it is their *characters* which need some overhauling. Many years ago, I learned from personal observation that the expert in prophecy is not always an example in piety! But he ought to be! This is the whole thrust of Peter's exhortation when he writes, "Seeing then that all these things shall be dissolved, what manner of persons ought ye to be in all holy conversation and godliness" (2 Pe 3:11).

What kind of people should we be? To begin with, if our belief in the imminent return of Jesus Christ is current, then we will be *careful* how we live. This was the substance of John's counsel when he wrote to the family of God, "Beloved, now are we the sons of God, and it doth not yet appear what we shall be: but we know that, when he shall appear, we shall be like him; for we shall see him as he is. And every man that hath this hope in him purifieth himself, even as he is pure" (1 Jn 3:2-3).

It was Paul's responsibility to write out in some detail just what this involves. Again and again, he presses this point. In one of Scripture's classic passages, the apostle spares noth-

ing to remind us that those who preach the blessed hope
should practice the blessed holiness! After describing the
believer's union with Christ now and hereafter, he goes on to
make his appeal in these solemn words,

> Mortify, therefore, your members which are upon the earth:
> fornication, uncleanness, inordinate affection, evil desire,
> and covetousness (which is idolatry), for which things' sake
> the wrath of God cometh on the sons of disobedience; in the
> which ye also once walked, when ye lived in them. But now
> ye also put off all these: anger, wrath, malice, blasphemy,
> filthy communication out of your mouth. Lie not one to
> another, seeing that ye have put off the old man with his
> deeds, and have put on the new man, that is renewed in
> knowledge after the image of him that created him; where
> there is neither Greek nor Jew, circumcision nor uncircumci-
> sion, barbarian, Scythian, bond nor free, but Christ is all, and
> in all (Col 3:5-11, NSRB).

Mind you, this is but one sample of many which teach that
practical piety and personal purity are consonant with a
belief in the coming of our Lord. Indeed, these passages
serve as inspired checklists to which we would do well to
repair from time to time.

Peter Marshall related the story of the pastor who visited a
young mother whose first child had been born. She was a
modern girl, and her home was about average for young
married couples. As the pastor entered the hospital room, he
found the young mother propped up in bed writing.

"'Come in,'" she said, smiling, "'I'm in the midst of
house-cleaning, and I want your help. . . .I've had a wonder-
ful chance to think here, . . .and it may help me to get things
straightened out in my mind if I talk to you.'" She put down
her pencil and pad, and folded her hands. Then she took a
long breath and started:

"'Ever since I was a little girl, I hated any sort of restraint.
I always wanted to be free. When I finished high school, I
took a business course and got a job—not because I needed

the money—but because I wanted to be on my own.

"'Before Joe and I were married, we used to say that we would not be slaves to each other. And after we married our apartment became headquarters for a crowd just like us. . . . We did what we pleased.'

"She stopped for a minute and smiled ruefully.

"'God didn't mean much to us—we ignored Him. . . . Things are different now. I'm not free any more, and I don't want to be. And the first thing I must do is clean house.'"

"With that, she picked up the pencil and pad lying on the counterpane, and turning to the pastor, she said, 'That's my house-cleaning list. You see, when I take Betty home from the hospital with me—our apartment will be her home—not just mine and Joe's.

"'And it isn't fit for her now. Certain things will have to go—for Betty's sake. And I've got to house-clean my heart and mind. I'm not just myself—I'm Betty's mother: And that means I need God. . . . Won't you pray for Betty and me and Joe, and for our new home?'"[2]

It should be no less with us! Every time we read a promise concerning the Lord's coming and our gathering unto Him in that house of many "apartments," let us pause long enough to make certain that we are fit to go there.

What manner of men ought we to be? *Careful!*

There is a second vital matter. If our belief in the Lord's return is relevant, we will be *considerate* of one another. A very warm human-interest story lies behind the apostolic letter to the church at Philippi. That little mission church in the city was the delight of Paul's heart. But like all assemblies where there are people—God's people—there were problems, primarily in the area of human relations. It seems clear that in that church there were two prominent women who had literally wrestled with the apostle in the proclamation of the gospel but now were wrestling with each other over some personal problem. While we are not told specifically what the problem was, we may draw an inference from the names of these sisters in Christ. Euodias was the well-

to-do one of the pair, while Syntyche was the better mixer.
So their names suggest. In any event, they had a head-on
collision, and the damage was so serious that Paul felt constrained to speak to each of them about it. The exhortation
occurs in the opening words of chapter 4, where he be-
seeches Euodias and Syntyche to be of the same mind in the
Lord. And on what basis? "Let your moderation be known
unto all men. The Lord is at hand" (Phil 4:5).

Practical Paul was pleading with this pair to stop their
sisterly squabble long enough to ask themselves the only
sensible question when a misunderstanding arises among the
saints: What difference will it make when the Lord comes?

Over the decades of my own ministry, I have often
thought to myself, *What a difference there would be in many
a church fellowship if believers could only be more considerate of one another.* But alas, as David Donald in his history
of the Civil War put it, *Divided We Fought!*

What manner of persons ought we to be? *Considerate!*

There is a third matter. In the light of His coming soon, we
will be *comforted* in the loss of loved ones who have passed
into the presence of their Lord. How thankful we should be
that the young church met nearly every problem facing believers in any generation, so that we hold in sacred trust
considerable inspired counsel on many matters. This includes the truth of the Lord's return.

As we know, although Paul spent less than a month in
Thessalonica, he ranged over many important truths related
to the Christian life. In his teaching on the coming of Christ,
it is quite clear that he distinguished the resurrections, as the
Scriptures declare, rather than teaching one general resurrection. The believers received this truth as vital to their
newfound faith. But a problem developed for which they
lacked suitable advice. In which of the various chapters of
the resurrection would their saved loved ones, now dead, be
raised? Believing, as they apparently did, that they might be
caught up at any moment, were they to conclude that their
loved ones must await another gathering at another time? It

was in answer to that pressing question that the apostle wrote in the fullest manner regarding the rapture of the church and those who would participate in it. This is what he wrote to his troubled, concerned friends:

> But I would not have you to be ignorant, brethren, concerning them who are asleep, that ye sorrow not, even as others who have no hope. For if we believe that Jesus died and rose again, even so them also who sleep in Jesus will God bring with him. For this we say unto you by the word of the Lord, that we who are alive and remain unto the coming of the Lord shall not precede them who are asleep. For the Lord himself shall descend from heaven with a shout, with the voice of the archangel, and with the trump of God; and the dead in Christ shall rise first; then we who are alive and remain shall be caught up together with them in the clouds, to meet the Lord in the air; and so shall we ever be with the Lord. Wherefore, comfort one another with these words (1 Th 4:13-18, NSRB).

What manner of persons ought we to be? *Comforted!*

The evidence is gathering. What kind of people should we be in the expectation that Jesus may come today? Be careful. Be considerate. Be comforted. And be *cheered* about these bodies of ours, which are so evidently showing signs of their temporality and need a change. Already, certain changes have begun for the child of God. "If any man be in Christ, he is a new creature: old things have passed away; behold, all things are become new" (2 Co 5:17). Our new life in Christ, then, has brought about a changed nature. Old critters have become new creatures! The same apostle, writing to the believers in the church at Rome, challenged them to present their bodies a living sacrifice, holy, acceptable unto God, which was their reasonable service. And to be not conformed to this world, but transformed by the renewing of their minds, so that they might demonstrate that good, and acceptable, and perfect will of God (Ro 12:1-2). From this, we learn that we may have a changed *mind.*

Only one thing is lacking. We need a changed *body*! But

never fear, this, too, is promised as we await our Lord's return from heaven. To that little flock at Philippi, Paul wrote, "For our conversation is in heaven; from whence also we look for the Saviour, the Lord Jesus Christ: who shall change our vile body, that it may be fashioned like unto his glorious body, according to the working whereby he is able even to subdue all things unto himself" (Phil 3:20-21).

The memories come flooding in of the many people who went home to the Lord during my years in the ministry. It was my custom on such occasions to take my place beside the remains of the loved one as the mortician prepared the body for its journey to the cemetery. Often I observed with interest as the man in charge removed the glasses of the deceased and carefully placed them beside the body so they would be handy for use next time. My own heart always reacted to that thoughtful gesture. I knew the funeral director was doing his work as considerately as possible, but I always had to say to myself, *My friend, when the Lord returns and he gets up, he won't need those!*

And why not? "We shall all be changed!" That's how it will be when Jesus comes again. And that is why we sing with Ada Habershon.

> Soon will our Savior from heaven appear,
> Sweet is the hope and its power to cheer;
> All will be changed by a glimpse of His face—
> This is the goal at the end of our race.
>
>> Oh, what a change!
>> Oh, what a change!
>> When I shall see His wonderful face!
>> Oh, what a change!
>> Oh, what a change!
>> When I shall see His face!

A little lad sitting in the door of his mountain cabin was asked by a passerby, "Son, do you live here?"

"Yes," he replied, "but we've a new home up the hill, and

we're moving tomorrow. You can see farther! The water's better! And everything is brand new!"

What manner of persons ought we to be? *Cheered!*

And now, finally, a relevant attitude toward the Lord's soon coming will produce a loving *concern* for those still without Christ.

> It does no good [writes Vance Havner] to revel among the clouds of prophetic truth if it stir us not to practice it on the cobblestones, questing for souls. . . . Prophetic truth, like all other truth, should be fuel for the fires of evangelism. . . . It is not enough to lament the apostasy so vividly described in the book of Jude. It is not even enough to build up ourselves in the faith, pray in the Holy Ghost, keep ourselves in the love of God, and look for the mercy of the Lord. There is a further duty: "And of some have compassion, making a difference: and other save with fear, pulling them out of the fire: hating even the garment spotted by the flesh."[3]

During the reign of Oliver Cromwell, the government ran out of silver for coins. Cromwell sent his men to the cathedral to see if they could find any there. They reported, "The only silver we can find is in the statues of the saints standing in the corners." To which the great soldier and statesman of England replied, "Good, we'll melt down the saints, and put them in circulation!"

What manner of persons ought we to be? *Concerned!*

When we are burdened for the lost, who are without God and without hope in this world and the world to come, we may expect not only that some will believe unto eternal life, but that in some measure we are fulfilling the purpose for which He is pleased to leave us here a little longer!

It was a fitting tribute that Zebah and Zalmunna paid to Gideon when he asked them, "What manner of men were they whom ye slew at Tabor? And they answered, As thou art, so were they; each one resembled the children of a king" (Judg 8:18).

May this be our witness in the world.

16
The Top of the Hill

INTERNATIONAL EVENTS in recent months have given us
some additional words for our working vocabulary. One
which has been in frequent circulation, primarily because of
our chief executive's visits abroad, is the word *summitry*. By
simplest definition, it means the top!

This present international posture has a future, spiritual
counterpart. I speak of *heaven's* summit conference. Whatever we may have thought about this, the solemn fact is that
such a conference is inevitable. It is so because judgment is
an essential part of biblical religion. "In both the Old and
New Testaments it inevitably arises out of the nature of God
as righteous. A righteous God must judge sin and reward
obedience." Thus observed Walter W. Wessel.

Throughout this series of meditations, we have confined
our thoughts to the various aspects of the *believer's* walk
along the journey. In this final chapter, whatever is dis-
cussed is set in the framework of the Christian's relationship
to that next great event on the agenda immediately following
the rapture of the Church of God into heaven. The Bible
speaks of that event as the judgment seat of Christ and
mentions it in two primary passages. In Romans 14:10-12,
we read, "But why dost thou judge thy brother? or why dost
thou set at nought thy brother? for we shall all stand before
the judgment seat of Christ. For it is written, As I live, saith
the Lord, every knee shall bow to me, and every tongue shall
confess to God. So then every one of us shall give account of
himself to God." And again, in 2 Corinthians 5:9-10, we read
these words, "Wherefore we labour, that, whether present

or absent, we may be accepted of him. For we must all appear before the judgment seat of Christ; that every one may receive the things done in his body, according to that he hath done, whether it be good or bad."

Before we examine this particular aspect of Christian truth, we should make several general observations which it provokes. In the first place, this judgment is not a *general* judgment for everyone. The context of the two passages cited earlier makes it clear that the apostle, by his use of the words *we all*, is addressing himself only to believers. This judgment will be strictly a family affair. There will be another judgment for the unbelievers, to be sure; this is spoken of in Revelation 20:11 as the judgment of the great white throne. At that judgment, only the non-Christian will appear, judged solely because his name "was not found written in the book of life" (Rev 20:15). The second critical fact to keep in perspective about the judgment seat of Christ is that this judgment will be concerned only with rewards for faithful service. It has nothing whatever to do with the subject of one's salvation; that matter was settled long before! As Handley Moule so aptly defines it, "The question to be tried and decided (speaking after the manner of men) at His 'tribunal,' in this reference, is not that of glory or perdition; the persons of the examined are accepted; the enquiry is in the *domestic* court of the Palace, so to speak; it regards the award of the King as to the issues and value of His accepted servants' labour and conduct, as His representatives, in their mortal life."[1]

But I can imagine someone raising the question just here: Why a judgment at all for the Christian? Isn't that all in the past? Of necessity, the answer has a yes and a no. It is true that judgment for us as *sinners* is past! Scripture could not be clearer on that point. "Verily, verily, I say unto you, He that heareth my word, and believeth on him that sent me, hath everlasting life, and shall not come into condemnation [or judgment]; but is passed from death unto life" (Jn 5:24). "There is therefore now no condemnation [judgment] to

them who are in Christ Jesus" (Ro 8:1). We may with
assurance sing with Horatio Spafford,

> My sin—oh, the bliss of this glorious thought,
> My sin—not in part, but the whole,
> Is nailed to the cross and I bear it no more,
> Praise the Lord, praise the Lord, O my soul!

It was Thomas a Kempis who once said, "The sign of the
cross shall be in heaven when the Lord cometh to judgment." And so it will!

But, you see, the Christian is something more than a
sinner, converted and cleansed from his sin. In his present
condition, he is now a *son* of God. And in that relationship,
he is subject to the duties and disciplines of a heavenly
Father. It was to this aspect of the believer's life that the
Holy Spirit addressed Himself when He said, "My son,
despise not thou the chastening of the Lord, nor faint when
thou art rebuked of him: for whom the Lord loveth he chas-
teneth, and scourgeth every son whom he receiveth. If ye
endure chastening, God dealeth with you as with sons"
(Heb 12:5-7). God has standards for His family, and He
expects His sons to behave. When they choose to be disobe-
dient, He judges them as sons so that they might not be
condemned with the world. While every Christian is fit for
heaven, he may not necessarily be fit for earth!

The Word of God distinguishes yet a third aspect of the
believer's life, and it is this aspect which brings us to the
really vital matter of this meditation. We speak now of the
child of God, not as one who was a sinner, nor even as a son,
but as a *steward*. I shall not soon forget how this word took
hold of my heart some years ago while reading the gospel of
Luke. In one place, our Lord is speaking to His disciples,
and says, "There was a certain rich man, which had a
steward; and the same was accused unto him that he had
wasted his goods. And he called him, and said unto him,
How is it that I hear this of thee? give an account of thy

stewardship" (Lk 16:1-2). Those last five words gripped my soul in a new way, for I realized that the Saviour's words to His steward in the story would be the Saviour's words to me one day. It is that thought which makes the judgment seat of Christ so solemn.

Having established the base of the coming judgment for every Christian as to his stewardship, let us give careful attention to three aspects of that stewardship.

In 1 Corinthians 4:1-2, the apostle writes as follows: "Let a man so account of us, as of the ministers of Christ, and stewards of the mysteries of God." Now, in the New Testament sense, a steward is one who holds in sacred trust the management of another's household goods. This raises an important question with far-reaching implications. The question is, What are some of these goods with which the believer has been entrusted? If we can ascertain that, then we may be in a position to fulfill our responsibility.

Let us begin by reminding ourselves that we are stewards of these *bodies* of ours. They are His by creation. They are His by purchase. Therefore, "glorify God in your body, and in your spirit, which are God's" (1 Co 6:20). I am not at liberty to use or abuse my body as I choose; I belong to another.

Furthermore, we are stewards of our *time*. As we carefully consider time's brevity, its opportunity, and its utility, we will appreciate, in some measure at least, Paul's words to the Ephesians: "See then that ye walk circumspectly, not as fools, but as wise; redeeming the time, because the days are evil" (Eph 5:15-16). For the Christian to say that he is "killing time" is to impugn his calling as a steward.

We are also stewards of our *grace gifts*. Distribution of these gifts has been made to every believer. They are to be exercised in the church for the proper function of the body, and for the purpose of equipping the saints for their ministry in effecting the maturity of the body of Christ, the Church. It is when these gifts are recognized and exercised that the Church prospers in her worship and witness.

Yet once more, we are stewards of our *money*. It is a fact of biblical revelation that our Lord had more to say about the acquisition and distribution of material means than about any other single subject. There was a reason for that. He saw with what difficulty men were able to handle their earthly possessions without being possessed by them! It has been wisely observed by William Elliott, Jr., in *Lift High that Banner*, "We own nothing, but are tenants of our room on earth, borrowers of wealth and implements, which must be returned; we inherit, use, and leave behind, but we possess nothing, except as trusted stewards who shall give account to him that giveth all."

At this point, we should have some better understanding of what our stewardship involves and some appreciation of what Peter had in mind when he admonished the saints to be "good stewards of the manifold grace of God" (1 Pe 4:10). What privileges and responsibilities are ours as stewards of God!

Now the issue is simply this, What test will the judgment seat of Christ require of us? In a word, *faithfulness*. Paul says, "It is required in stewards, that a man be found faithful" (1 Co 4:2). Not successful, just faithful. Erich Sauer, in referring to this standard of our faithfulness and its exposure at the judgment seat, sees it as

> the sum total of our life, the product of our development: not only our deeds but also our possibilities, not only what we were but what we might have become, not only our actions but also our omissions (Jas 4:17); not the work but the worker, not the number but the weight of our deeds (1 Sam 2:3); not only what we attained but also what we strove after. Of our works, sacrifice counts for most; of our disposition, only selfless love; of our possessions, only what we employed in service. . .in everything He will take note of the most inward elements, of the impulses and motives, of the counsels of the heart, of the secrets of the soul hidden in darkness.[2]

Thank God, Paul assures us that in the end "shall every man

have praise of God" (1 Co 4:5). The faithful One will find something worthy of commendation in every believer's life.

A second aspect of our stewardship occurs in 1 Corinthians 3:11-15.

> For other foundation can no man lay than that is laid, which is Jesus Christ. Now if any man build upon this foundation gold, silver, precious stones, wood, hay, stubble; every man's work shall be made manifest: for the day shall declare it, because it shall be revealed by fire; and the fire shall try every man's work of what sort it is. If any man's work abide which he hath built thereupon, he shall receive a reward. If any man's work shall be burned, he shall suffer loss: but he himself shall be saved; yet so as by fire.

Mark well here that the *foundation* is not our concern. That has already been laid by our Lord Jesus Christ. What does concern us, however, is the *superstructure*. "Let every man take heed how he buildeth thereupon" (v. 10).

It is interesting to observe that the words "judgment seat," in the original language, suggest a raised place on which the magistrate sat to hear legal cases. It was a tribunal or as the original suggests, a "footprint." At this footprint tribunal, our footprints through this life will be examined to see where and how we have walked. Quite obviously from the text, the footprints will be varied. Some will show the marks of permanency, as indicated by the gold, silver, and precious stones; others will reveal signs of that which is perishable, as suggested by the wood, hay, and stubble. The important thing to bear in mind is that that day will determine *which*—not how much, but what kind! So, the appeal here is to carefulness as to the materials which we accumulate in anticipation of our appointment.

I recall the story of a Christian woman who had a dream. In her dream, she found herself being transported about the streets of heaven. Passing one mansion after another, she came to a very magnificent one which the celestial courier identified as that of her lowly servant in her home on earth. She thought to herself, *If this is what he has, what must mine be like!*

She was not long getting her answer, for the driver turned down a modest road to a little place which was hardly worthy of notice, compared to the other. This provoked an immediate response. "I don't quite understand. How is it that my servant has such a fine place, and I must be content with this?"

Whereupon the heavenly guide replied, "Madam, we did the best we could with what you sent us!"

Paul was not overstating the case, was he, when he wrote, "Let every man take heed how he buildeth thereupon!" Carefulness is the challenge.

A third aspect of our stewardship is found in 1 Corinthians 9:24-27.

> Know ye not that they which run in a race run all, but one receiveth the prize? So run, that ye may obtain. And every man that striveth for the mastery is temperate in all things. Now they do it to obtain a corruptible crown; but we an incorruptible. I therefore so run, not as uncertainly; so fight I, not as one that beateth the air: But I keep under my body, and bring it into subjection: lest that by any means, when I have preached to others, I myself should be a castaway.

Bear in mind that Paul is not talking about a struggle for salvation; that matter was settled, as we remarked earlier. Rather, it is a race for rewards. Paul's term for it is *crown*, and there are a number of crowns cited in the Word. There is the crown of rejoicing (1 Th 2:19), the crown of righteousness (2 Ti 4:8), the crown of life (Ja 1:12), the crown of glory (1 Pe 5:4), and the crown of incorruption referred to in our present text.

To the mind of the apostle, drawing his imagery from the Isthmian games, the Christian life was a race. It was a race with a finish, and it promised a reward to the victor. With these things before him, he considered that nothing should be spared. Every nerve should be strained to win through to victory. Accordingly, he disciplined himself by avoiding anything—bodily desires especially—which might hinder his running the course so that he might win the crown!

In a word, he was the picture of resoluteness. Paul was a disciplined, determined man! "I therefore so run." This is his example for us.

The judgment seat of Christ awaits the catching away of the church. There the records will be examined, and each of us will give an account of himself to the Lord. The scrutiny of that tribunal will not concern the corporate company of the redeemed, but each member, each man. As Bishop Moule wrote in his commentary on Romans, "Each will stand in a solemn solitude there, before his divine Examiner. What *he* was, as the Lord's member, that will be the question. What *he* shall be, as such, in the functions of the endless state, that will be the result."[4]

And the issues again? Faithfulness. Carefulness. And resoluteness.

Little wonder that the apostle John, in his last days, wrote to the elect lady, "Look to yourselves, that we lose not those things which we have wrought, but that we receive a full reward" (2 Jn 8). The very thought of such a challenge should nerve our faint endeavor and cause us to say with Amy Carmichael, "The vows of God are upon me. I may not stay to play with shadows or pluck earthly flowers, till I my work have done, and rendered up account."

But alas! I fear it will not be so with many. They will be like the parishioner who, hearing his pastor's message on this subject, confessed, "Pastor, I'm not afraid to die. But I'm ashamed to die!"

It is still not too late. We are not yet at the top of the hill. Let us take to ourselves the clarion call of Charles Wesley, who wrote,

A charge to keep I have,
A God to glorify,

A never-dying soul to save,
And fit it for the sky.

To serve the present age,
My calling to fulfill;
O may it all my powers engage,
To do my Master's will!

Arm me with jealous care,
As in Thy sight to live,
And O Thy servant, Lord, prepare,
A strict account to give.

That will be the top of the hill! And our shoes will have brought us there.

Notes

Grateful acknowledgment is given the sources listed below, which have been a great asset in the preparation of these meditations. Much effort has been taken to identify and include as many as possible, and apology is extended to any that may have been omitted.

PROLOGUE
1. Frank W. Boreham, *Faces in the Fire* (New York: Abingdon, 1919), p. 263.

CHAPTER 1
1. William Law, *A Serious Call to a Devout and Holy Life*, ed. and abr. John W. Meister (Philadelphia: Westminster, 1968), p. 29-30. Copyright MCMLV, by W. L. Jenkins. Used by permission of The Westminster Press.
2. Amy Carmichael, "Make Me Thy Fuel," in *Amy Carmichael of Dohnavur*, Frank Houghton (London: SPCK, 1953), p. 36. Used by permission of the publisher.

CHAPTER 2
1. A. J. Gordon, *How Christ Came to Church*, (Philadelphia: Am. Bap. Pub. Soc., 1895), pp. 4-7.
2. J. H. Jowett, *The Transfigured Church*, (New York: Revell, 1910), p. 19.

CHAPTER 3
1. W. Hone, in F. B. Meyer, *Paul, A Servant of Jesus Christ*, (London: Marshall, Morgan & Scott, 1910), p. 55.
2. Vance Havner, *Rest Awhile* (New York: Revell, 1941), pp. 62-63.

CHAPTER 4
1. W. H. Griffith Thomas, *Genesis: A Devotional Commentary*, (Grand Rapids: Eerdmans, 1946), p. 262.

CHAPTER 5
1. Alexander Whyte, *Bible Characters* (London: Oliphants, 1952), p. 97.
2. Billy Rose, "Pitching Horsehoes." Dist. by Bell-McClure Syndicate, publishers. Used by permission.

CHAPTER 6
1. William M. Elliott, Jr., *For the Living of These Days* (Richmond: Knox, 1946), p. 113.
2. As quoted by ibid.
3. W. E. Sangster, "Daily Readings from W. E. Sangster."

CHAPTER 7
1. William Salmond, as quoted by Herbert Lockyer, *All the Parables of the Bible* (Grand Rapids: Zondervan, 1963), p. 9.
2. Stuart Holden, *Some Old Testament Parables* (London: Pickering & Inglis, n.d.), p. 48.
3. Ibid., p. 49.
4. Ibid., pp. 49-50.

CHAPTER 8
1. Armin Haeussler, *The Story of Our Hymns* (St. Louis: Eden, 1952), p. 311.
2. Handley C. G. Moule, *The Epistle to the Romans* (London: Pickering & Inglis, 1928), p. 403.

CHAPTER 9
1. C. H. Mackintosh, *Notes on the Book of Numbers* (New York: Loizeaux, 1946), pp. 178-79.
2. William M. J. Long, *Fowls of the Air* (Boston: Ginn & Co., 1901).

CHAPTER 10
1. David J. Beattie, *The Romance of Sacred Song* (London: Marshall, Morgan, & Scott, 1931), pp. 216-17.

CHAPTER 11
1. Richard Ellsworth Day, *Filled! With the Spirit* (Grand Rapids: Zondervan, 1938), p. 244.
2. As quoted by William Marion Elliott, *Coming to Terms with Life* (Richmond, Va.: John Knox, 1944), p. 118.

CHAPTER 12
1. Vance Havner, *It Is Toward Evening* (Old Tappan, N.J.: Revell, 1968), pp. 39-40.
2. William M. Elliott, Jr., unpublished manuscript.
3. Frank W. Boreham, *Cliffs of Opal* (London: Epworth, 1948), p. 111.
4. Arthur T. Pierson, *The Bible and Spiritual Life* (New York: Gospel Pub., n.d.), p. 377.
5. C. H. Mackintosh, "Bethany," in *Life and Times of David*, Miscellaneous Writings, vol. 6 (New York: Loizeaux, 1951), pp. 20-21.
6. W. E. Sangster, "Daily Readings from W. E. Sangster," *Why Jesus Never Wrote a Book* (London: Methodist Pub.,), pp. 47-48. Used by permission of the publisher.

CHAPTER 13
1. Frank W. Boreham, *Faces in the Fire* (New York: Abingdon, 1919), pp. 164-5.
2. Stephen Olford, *The River of the Spirit* (Old Tappan, N.J.: Revell, 1959), p. 97.
3. Skevington Wood, "The Plus of the Spirit," in *The Keswick Week 1962* (London: Marshall, Morgan, & Scott, 1962), p. 143.

CHAPTER 14
1. From *Life* Magazine's series on Ancient Greece, Copyright © 1963 Time Inc. Used with permission.
2. T. S. Eliot, "Choruses from 'The Rock'" *Collected Poems 1909-1962* (New York: Harcourt, Brace, Jovanovich, 1963). Used by permission of the publisher.
3. Vance Havner, *Hearts Afire* (Old Tappan, N.J.: Revell, 1952), pp. 109-10.

CHAPTER 15
1. T. S. Eliot, "The Hollow Men," *Collected Poems 1909-62* (New York: Harcourt, Brace. Jovanovich, 1963). Used by permission of the publisher.
2. Peter Marshall, *Mr. Jones, Meet the Master* (Old Tappan, N.J.: Revell, 1950), pp. 156-57.
3. Vance Havner, *Road to Revival* (New York: Revell, 1940), p. 82.

CHAPTER 16
1. Handley C. G. Moule, *The Epistle to the Romans*, p. 386.
2. Erich Sauer, *The Triumph of the Crucified* (London: Paternoster, 1951), p. 114.